## ESSENTIAL CHINESE CHARACTERS
# CHINESE WRITING FOR KIDS

WORKBOOK 3 — CHARACTERS 201-300

LingLing

www.linglingmandarin.com

Copyright © 2025 Ling He (LingLing Mandarin)

All rights reserved. No part of this book including audio material may be reproduced or used in any manner without written permission of the copyright owner. For more information, contact:

enquiries@linglingmandarin.com

FIRST EDITION

Editing by Xinrong Huo
Cover design by LingLing

www.linglingmandarin.com

# CONTENTS

## INTRODUCTION — 5
- Welcome — 5
- Radicals And Character Composition — 5
- Learning Chinese Is Fun — 5
- What's In The Book — 6
- Learn, Practice, Have Fun — 6

## CHINESE STROKES — 7
- Basic Strokes — 7
- Basic Writing Rules — 9

## CHARACTER COMPOSITION — 10
- How Chinese Characters Are Formed — 10

## CHINESE RADICALS — 15
- Learning More Radicals — 15
- Writing Practice — 16

## CHINESE CHARACTERS — 23
Your Next 100 Chinese Characters — 23

| | | |
|---|---|---|
| Giving And Taking | 买卖给送拿扔 | 24 |
| Requests And Permissions | 请让可否答把 | 27 |
| Thinking And Ability | 想要知识会能 | 30 |
| Emotions And Feelings | 喜厌爱恨笑哭乐气 | 33 |
| Body Parts | 头脸眼鼻嘴耳肩手脚腿心肚 | 37 |
| Personal Belongings | 书本包笔尺纸钱卡表球 | 43 |
| Transportation | 车船机铁 | 48 |
| Buildings And Rooms | 店馆楼房间室 | 50 |
| Places | 国家市园路街校院 | 53 |
| Tableware | 刀叉碗筷盘勺杯瓶 | 57 |
| Food | 米饭蛋肉果菜面饼 | 61 |
| Drinks | 茶酒汁奶 | 65 |
| Clothes | 衣鞋裙裤袜帽 | 67 |
| Social Relationships | 父母师生友同伴员 | 70 |

## RESOURCES — 74
- Access Audio — 74
- 300 Essential Chinese Characters Workbook Series — 74
- Writing Practice Books — 75
- Beginner Books — 75

| Character | Pinyin | English | Page | Character | Pinyin | English | Page |
|---|---|---|---|---|---|---|---|
| 买 | mǎi | to buy | 24 | 机 | jī | aircraft; machine | 49 |
| 卖 | mài | to sell | 24 | 铁 | tiě | rail; iron | 49 |
| 给 | gěi | to give | 25 | 店 | diàn | shop | 50 |
| 送 | sòng | to gift; to send | 25 | 馆 | guǎn | place (services) | 50 |
| 拿 | ná | to take | 26 | 楼 | lóu | building | 51 |
| 扔 | rēng | to throw | 26 | 房 | fáng | house | 51 |
| 请 | qǐng | to invite; please | 27 | 间 | jiān | room; space | 52 |
| 让 | ràng | to let; to make | 27 | 室 | shì | room; place | 52 |
| 可 | kě | to approve; yes | 28 | 国 | guó | nation; country | 53 |
| 否 | fǒu | to negate; no | 28 | 家 | jiā | home; family | 53 |
| 答 | dá | to answer | 29 | 市 | shì | city | 54 |
| 把 | bǎ | to give; handle | 29 | 园 | yuán | garden | 54 |
| 想 | xiǎng | to want; to miss | 30 | 路 | lù | road | 55 |
| 要 | yào | to want (intend) | 30 | 街 | jiē | street | 55 |
| 知 | zhī | to know | 31 | 校 | xiào | school | 56 |
| 识 | shí | to recognize | 31 | 院 | yuàn | institution | 56 |
| 会 | huì | can; will | 32 | 刀 | dāo | knife | 57 |
| 能 | néng | be able to | 32 | 叉 | chā | fork; cross | 57 |
| 喜 | xǐ | to like | 33 | 碗 | wǎn | bowl | 58 |
| 厌 | yàn | to dislike | 33 | 筷 | kuài | chopsticks | 58 |
| 爱 | ài | to love | 34 | 盘 | pán | plate | 59 |
| 恨 | hèn | to hate | 34 | 勺 | sháo | spoon | 59 |
| 哭 | kū | to cry | 35 | 杯 | bēi | cup; glass | 60 |
| 笑 | xiào | to laugh | 35 | 瓶 | píng | bottle | 60 |
| 乐 | lè | to cheer | 36 | 米 | mǐ | rice (raw) | 61 |
| 气 | qì | to be angry; air | 36 | 饭 | fàn | rice; meal | 61 |
| 头 | tóu | head | 37 | 蛋 | dàn | egg | 62 |
| 脸 | liǎn | face | 37 | 肉 | ròu | meat | 62 |
| 眼 | yǎn | eye | 38 | 果 | guǒ | fruit | 63 |
| 鼻 | bí | nose | 38 | 菜 | cài | vegetable; dish | 63 |
| 嘴 | zuǐ | mouth | 39 | 面 | miàn | flour; noodle | 64 |
| 耳 | ěr | ear | 39 | 饼 | bǐng | pie | 64 |
| 肩 | jiān | shoulder | 40 | 茶 | chá | tea | 65 |
| 手 | shǒu | hand | 40 | 酒 | jiǔ | wine | 65 |
| 脚 | jiǎo | foot | 41 | 汁 | zhī | juice | 66 |
| 腿 | tuǐ | leg | 41 | 奶 | nǎi | milk; grandma | 66 |
| 心 | xīn | heart | 42 | 衣 | yī | clothes | 67 |
| 肚 | dù | stomach | 42 | 鞋 | xié | shoes | 67 |
| 书 | shū | book | 43 | 裙 | qún | skirt; dress | 68 |
| 本 | běn | notebook | 43 | 裤 | kù | trousers | 68 |
| 包 | bāo | bag | 44 | 袜 | wà | socks | 69 |
| 笔 | bǐ | pen | 44 | 帽 | mào | hat | 69 |
| 尺 | chǐ | ruler | 45 | 父 | fù | father | 70 |
| 纸 | zhǐ | paper | 45 | 母 | mǔ | mother | 70 |
| 钱 | qián | money | 46 | 师 | shī | teacher | 71 |
| 卡 | kǎ | card | 46 | 生 | shēng | student; life | 71 |
| 表 | biǎo | watch | 47 | 友 | yǒu | friend | 72 |
| 球 | qiú | ball | 47 | 同 | tóng | same | 72 |
| 车 | chē | car; vehicle | 48 | 伴 | bàn | partner | 73 |
| 船 | chuán | boat; ship | 48 | 员 | yuán | staff | 73 |

# INTRODUCTION

## WELCOME

Welcome back to the **300 Essential Chinese Characters Workbook Series**! This is the third book in the series, where you'll take your skills to a higher level by learning to write 100 more Chinese characters. Completing this workbook, along with Workbooks 1 and 2, is a fantastic achievement—you'll have mastered 300 Chinese characters, an accomplishment few learners achieve!

## RADICALS AND CHARACTER COMPOSITION

In Workbooks 1 and 2, you mastered over 100 of the most common radicals and your first 200 Chinese characters, laying a strong foundation for your Chinese writing journey. In this book, you'll delve further into character composition with 26 examples, master 42 additional radicals, and learn 100 new characters.

## LEARNING CHINESE IS FUN

Chinese characters are very interesting because they are often pictographic, meaning many characters look like the things they represent. Learning and writing Chinese can be great fun as it can feel like drawing a simple picture or even solving the puzzle of why the character looks the way it does.

For example, the character for "rain" (雨) looks like raindrops falling from clouds. The character for "earth" (土) resembles a mound of soil, with the top stroke as the surface and the vertical line connecting it to the ground below. The character for "wood" (木) looks like a tall tree, with a central line as the trunk and branching strokes that spread out like its limbs.

# WHAT'S IN THE BOOK

In Chapter 1, you will review Chinese writing rules and the eight basic strokes, then further explore the rules of character composition and master 42 additional radicals. In Chapter 2, you will learn to write 100 new characters (Simplified Chinese, used in Mainland China), covering everyday topics such as clothes, places, body parts, transportation, activities, food, drinks, and more.

Each character includes:

- **Meaning** - What the character represents.
- **Pinyin** - How to pronounce it in Chinese.
- **Radical** - A clue to its meaning.
- **Stroke Order** - The correct way to write it beautifully.
- **Common Words** - Practical examples for everyday use.
- **Color Picture** - An engaging visual aid to help you remember the meaning.
- **FREE Downloadable Audio** - To help with pronunciation - check the **Access Audio** page to download.

With lots of space to practice, you'll trace each character and see your skills improve with every stroke! Step by step, you'll gain confidence, deepen your understanding, and lay a strong foundation for mastering Chinese. You're doing amazing! Keep going - you can do it!

## LEARN, PRACTICE, HAVE FUN

Learning Chinese is like planting a tree—each character you learn is like a seed that will grow into a tall, strong tree of knowledge. The more you practice, the better you'll get, just like the Chinese idiom:

# CHINESE STROKES

## BASIC STROKES

In the first book, you learnt these basic strokes. Here's a quick reminder of the eight basic Chinese strokes in Chinese writing, often called the "Eight Principles of Yong ( 永 )" because they can be seen in the character 永 (which means "forever"). Learning these eight strokes is important because they are the building blocks for all Chinese characters.

We've included all the information and practice space as in the first book; remember "repetition is the mother of learning," so why not take the opportunity to refresh your memory and practice a little more.

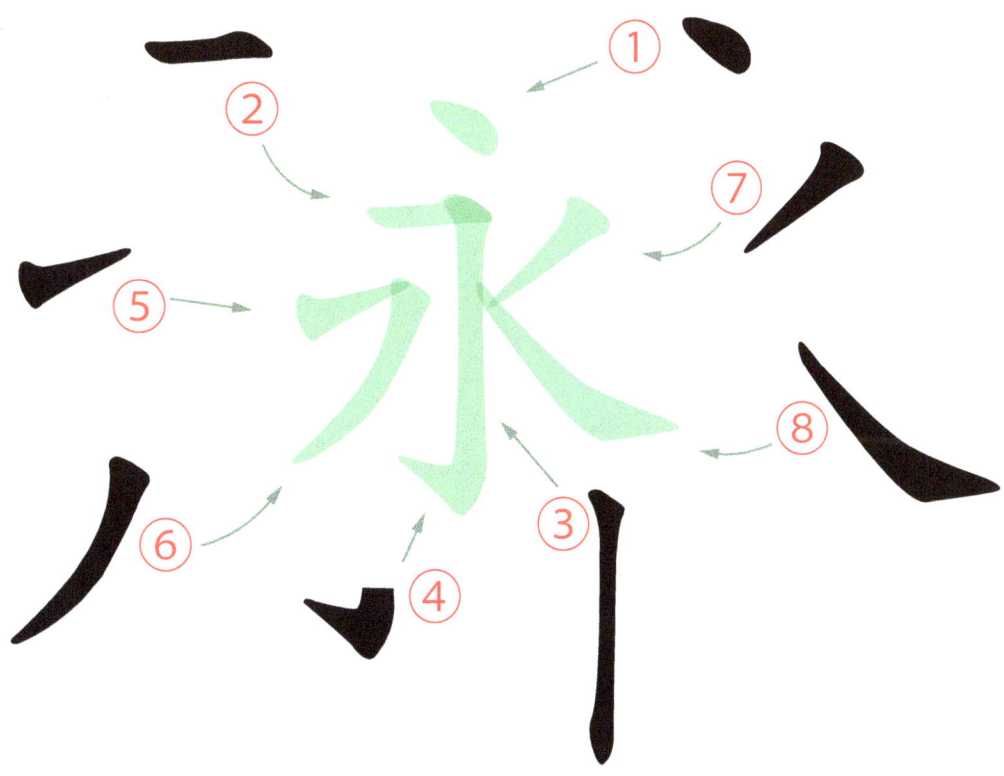

# BASIC WRITING RULES

When writing Chinese characters, there are some important rules to follow to ensure proper structure and balance. These rules will help you to write each stroke in the right order and will make writing easier and more straightforward, ensuring your characters remain neat and easy to read. If ever you forget, just come back here to refresh your memory!

## Top to Bottom

 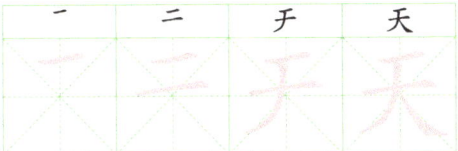 sky

## Left to Right

 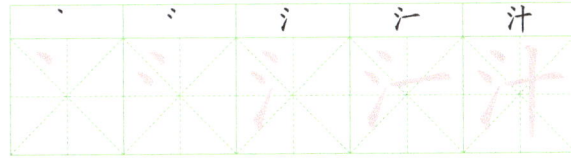 juice

## Horizontal, then Vertical

 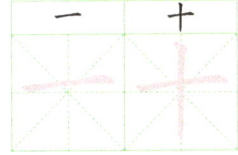 ten

## Left-falling, then Right-falling

 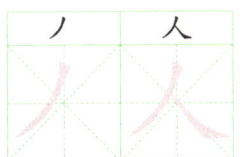 person

## Middle then Sides (when symmetrical)

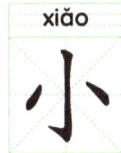 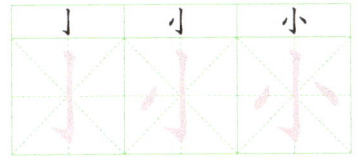 small

## Outside to Inside, then Close

 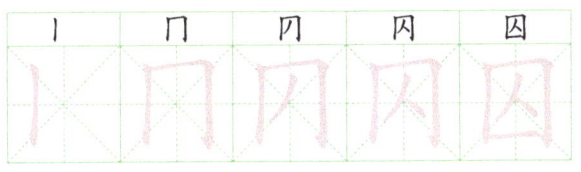 prisoner

# CHARACTER COMPOSITION

## HOW CHINESE CHARACTERS ARE FORMED

Chinese characters are fascinating puzzles, built from smaller pieces called components, each carrying a meaning or sound. By combining these components, new characters with unique meanings are formed.

In Workbooks 1 and 2, we explored over 100 common radicals, learning how they act as building blocks for creating characters. Radicals can either be smaller parts or independent characters themselves.

For example, the speech radical 讠 + 舌 (tongue) = 话 (speech or words), symbolizing the tongue working with speech to create spoken words.

Or, the grain radical/character 禾 + 火 (fire) = 秋 (autumn), symbolizing grains ripening under the sun's heat, marking the harvest season.

By understanding these "building blocks," you can often guess the meaning or pronunciation of unfamiliar characters, unlocking the secrets of Chinese writing! Let's take a look at some examples and practice writing the characters.

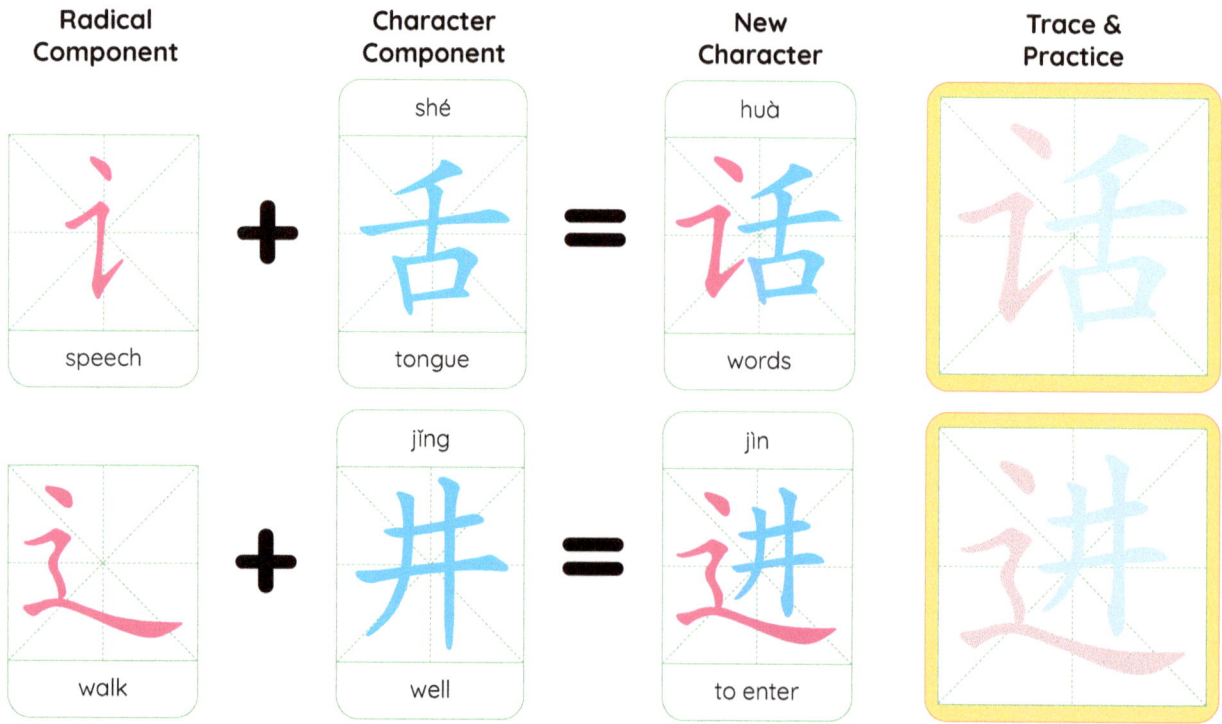

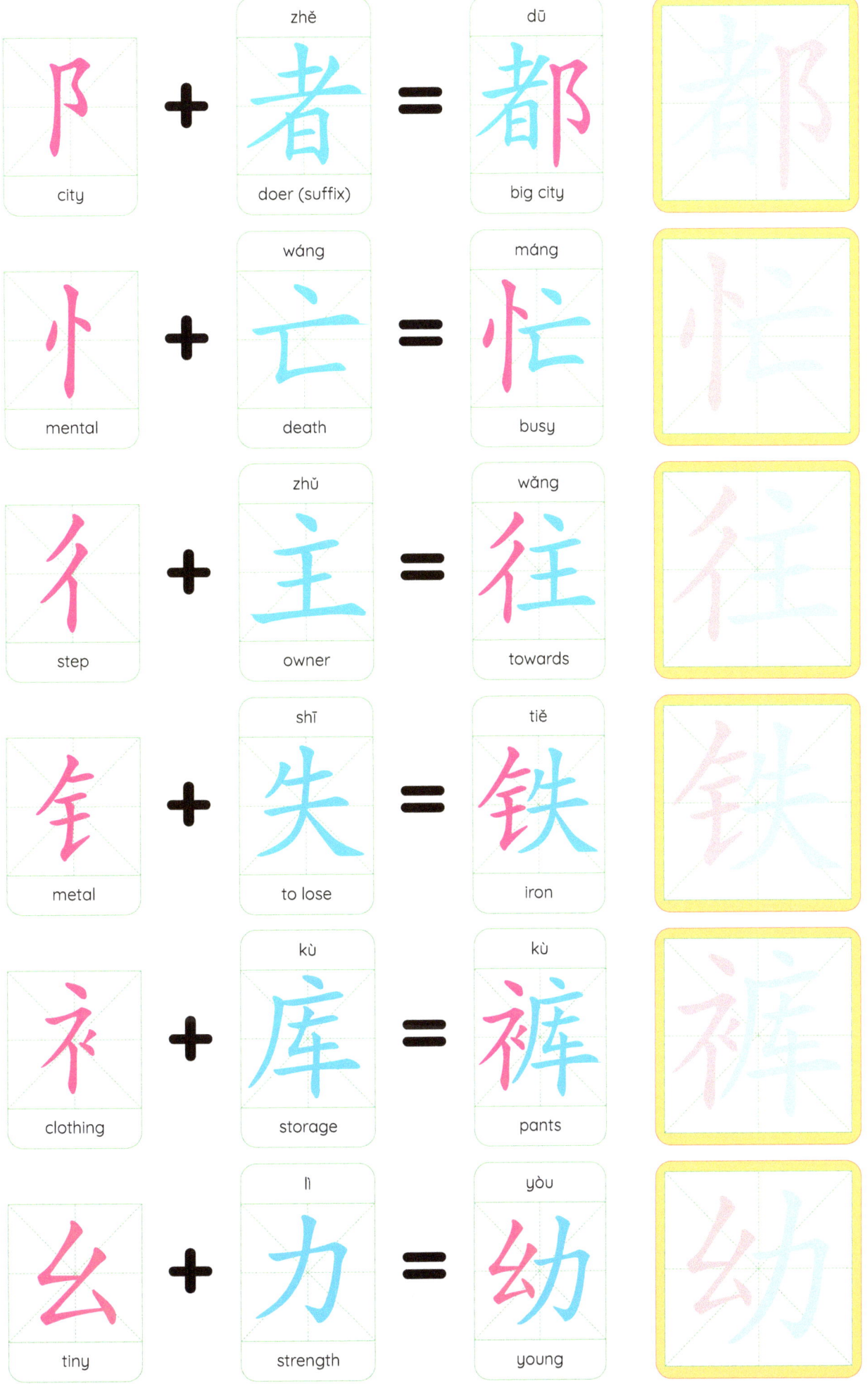

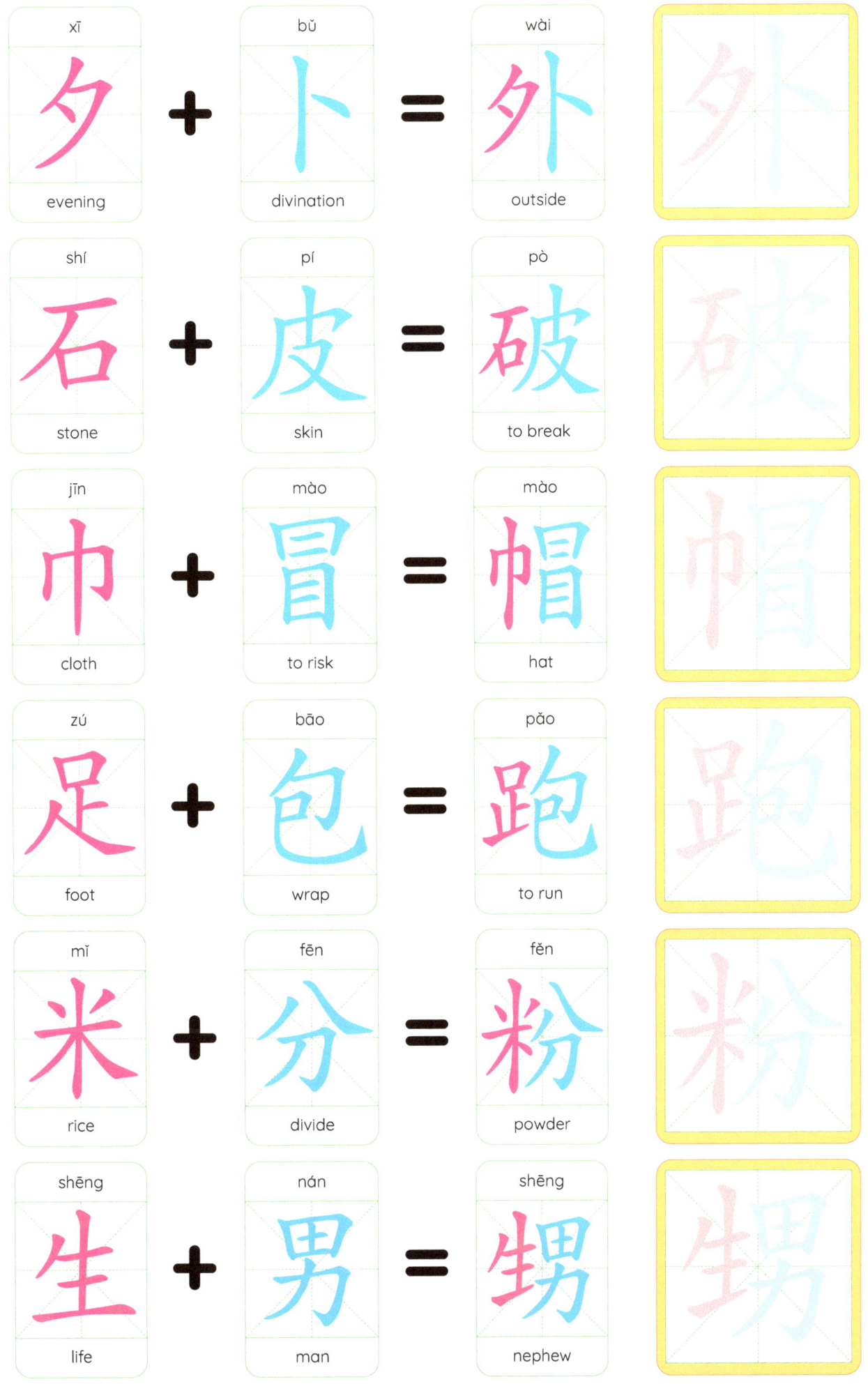

# CHINESE RADICALS

## LEARNING MORE RADICALS

In Workbooks 1 and 2, we learned 108 important radicals—the building blocks of Chinese characters! These little pieces often give us hints about what a character means. We also explored how these pieces fit together like a puzzle to make new characters.

Now, in Workbook 3, we'll meet 42 more radicals. Learning these will make it even easier to understand, guess, and remember Chinese characters. By the end of the workbook series, you'll know 150 radicals—almost all the ones you'll see in everyday Chinese! You'll also become a pro at figuring out how Chinese characters are built and connected.

Ready to begin? Follow the arrows and numbers to draw each radical step by step. Just focus on tracing the **radical** for now—don't worry about the whole character yet. We'll practice those later. Have fun and enjoy the adventure of learning Chinese writing!

- **A** Radical
- **B** Radical Meaning
- **C** Stroke Order
- **D** Stroke Direction
- **E** Example Character
- **F** Character Pinyin
- **G** Character Meaning
- **H** Trace the radical strokes in the example (shown in pink).

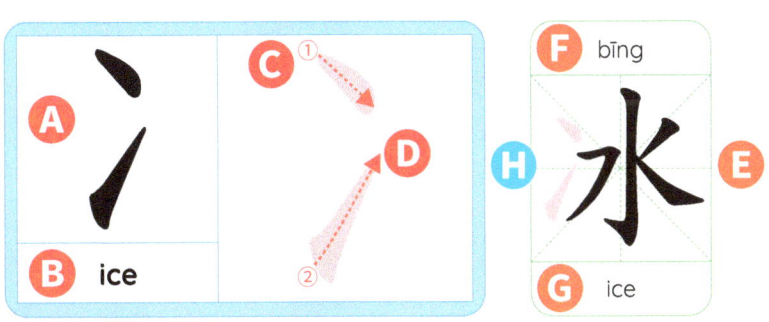

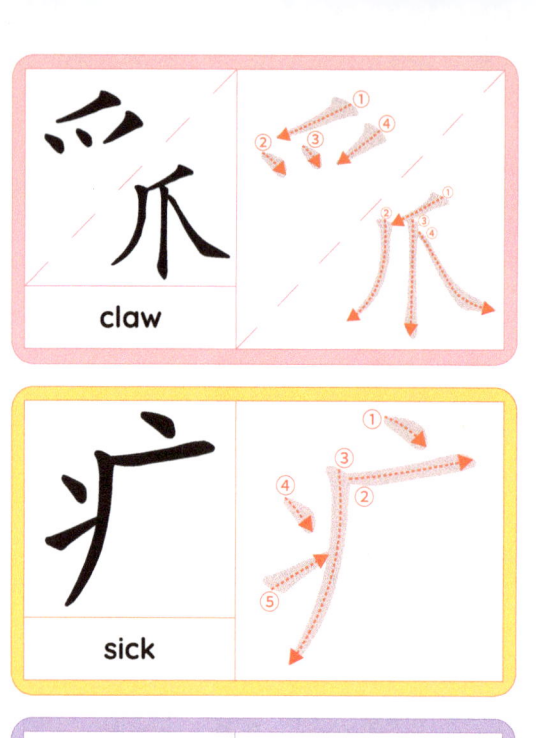
claw

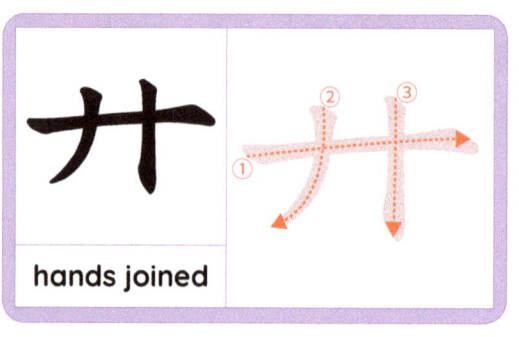
sick

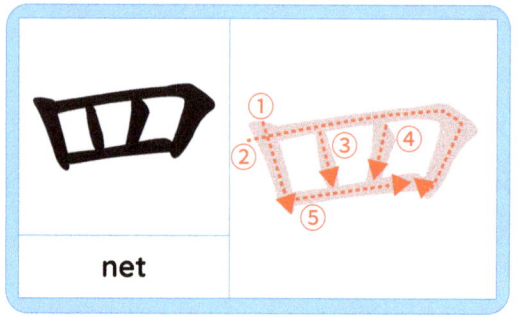
hands joined

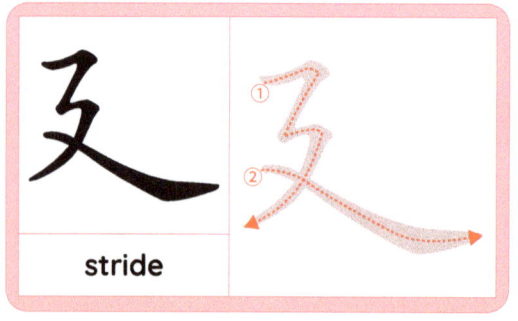
net

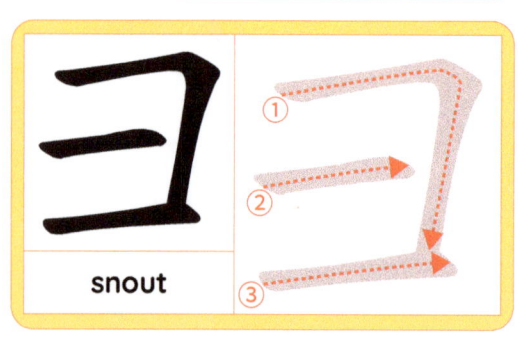
stride

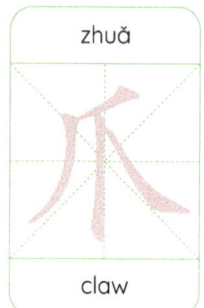
snout

| | | |
|---|---|---|
| zhuǎ  claw | pá 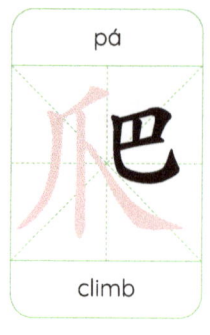 climb | ài  love |
| bìng  illness | liáo 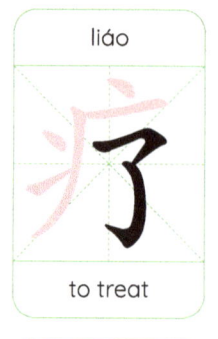 to treat | tòng  pain |
| kāi 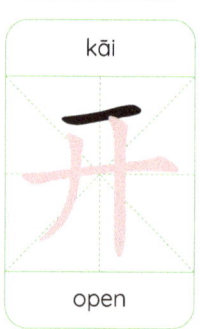 open | nòng 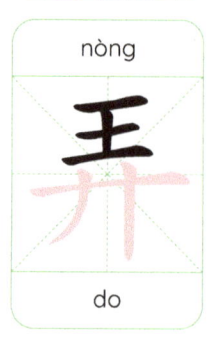 do | yì 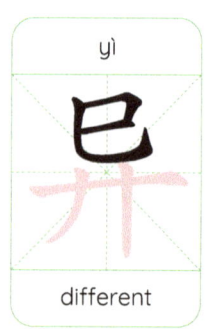 different |
| shǔ  Sichuan | luó 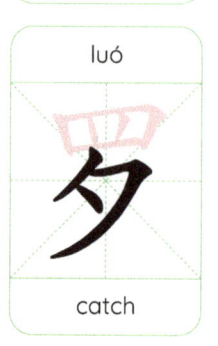 catch | zuì  crime |
| yán  extend | tíng  court | jiàn  build |
| dāng 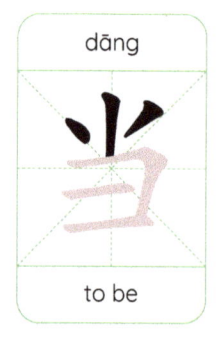 to be | huì  comet | zhǒu  broom |

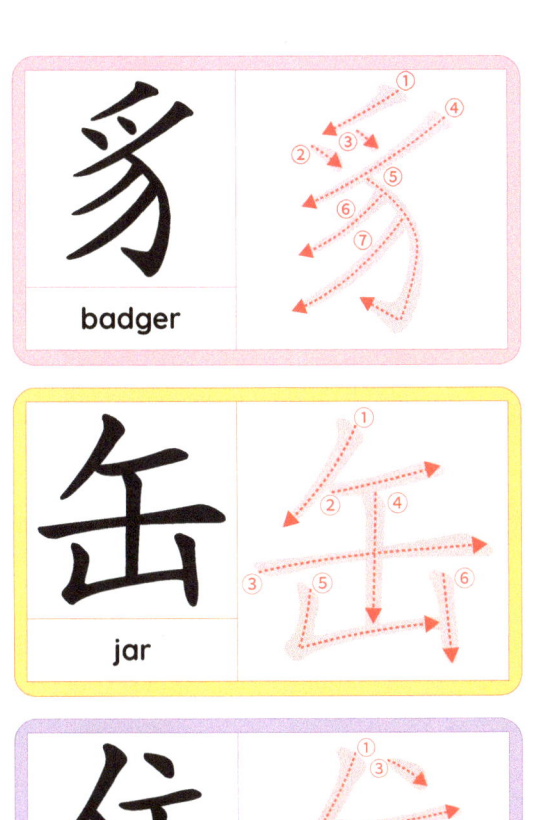
badger

bào
豹
leopard

mào
貌
appearance

diāo
貂
mink

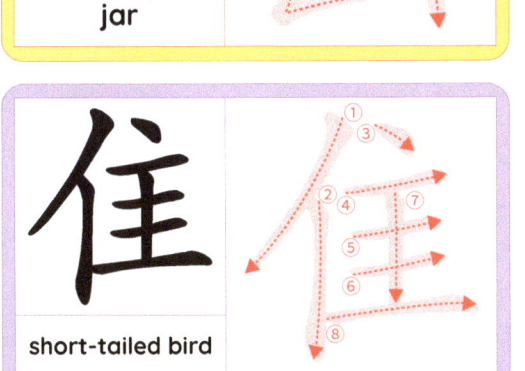
jar

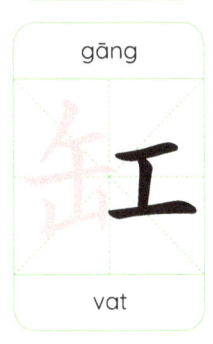
gāng
缸
vat

quē
缺
lack

guàn
罐
can (container)

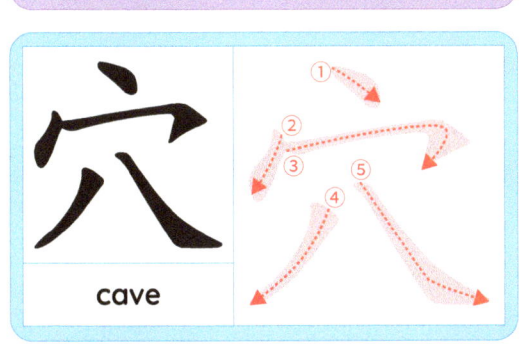
short-tailed bird

què
雀
sparrow

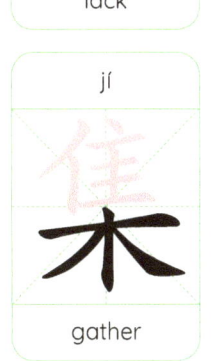
jí
集
gather

xióng
雄
hero

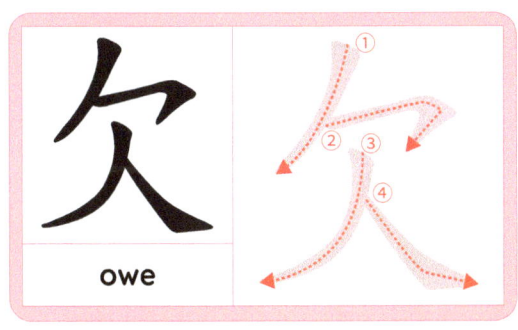
cave

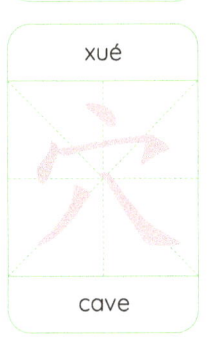
xué
穴
cave

kōng
空
empty

chuān
穿
through

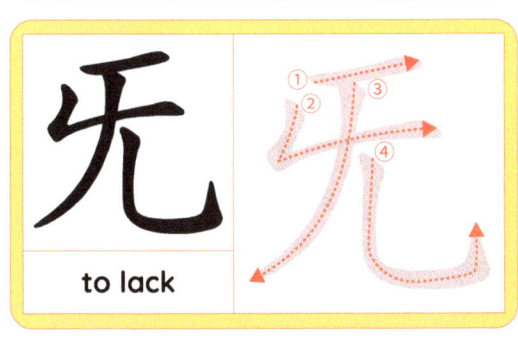
owe

qiàn
欠
owe

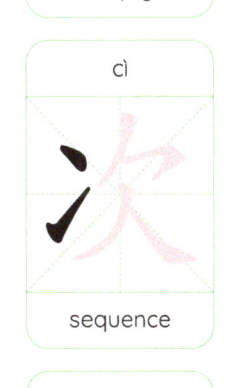
cì
次
sequence

gē
歌
song

to lack

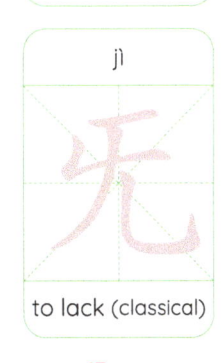
jì
旡
to lack (classical)

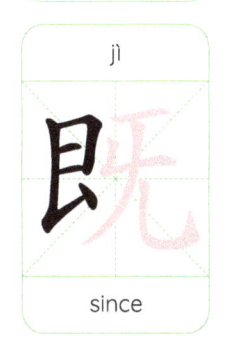
jì
既
since

jì
暨
reach

| 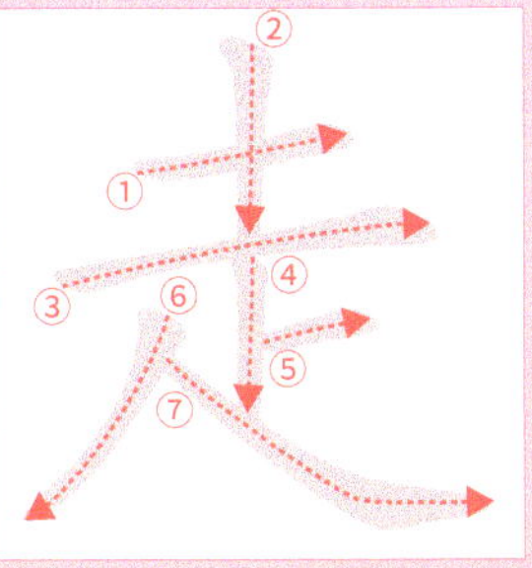 | zǒu 走 walk | qǐ 起 rise | yuè 越 cross over |
|---|---|---|---|
| 走 walk | | | |
| 羽 feather | 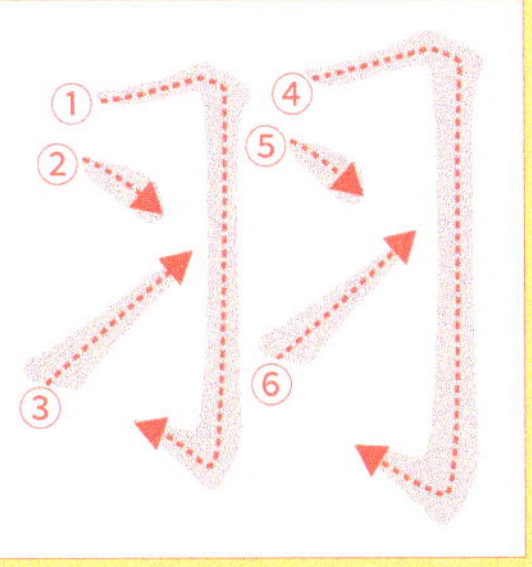 yǔ 羽 feather | xiáng 翔 soar | chì 翅 wing |
| 臼 mortar | 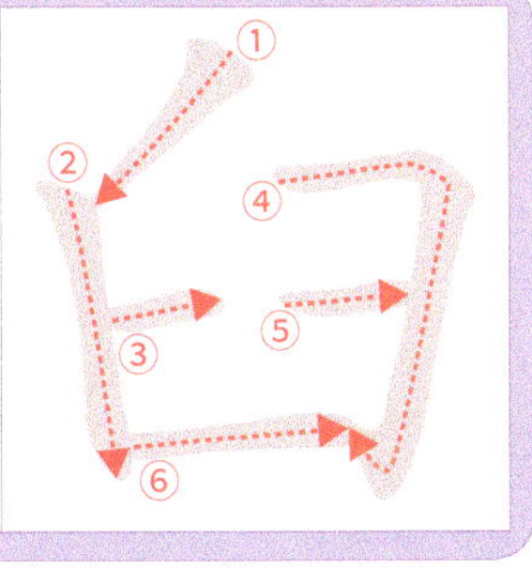 jiù 臼 mortar | jiù 舅 uncle | yú 臾 instant |
| 比 compare | 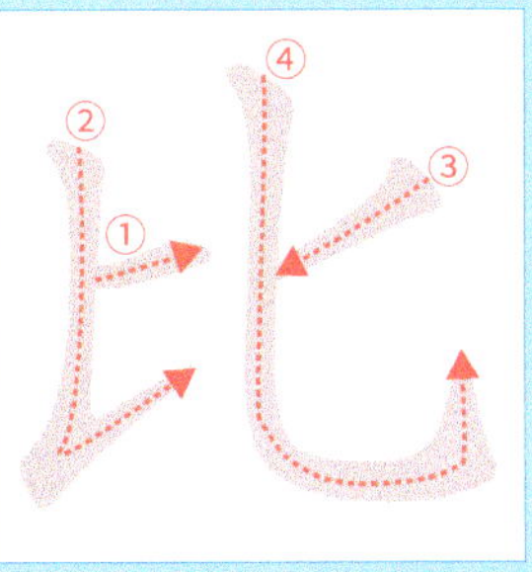 bǐ 比 compare | bì 毕 complete | bì 毙 to die |
| 甘 sweet | 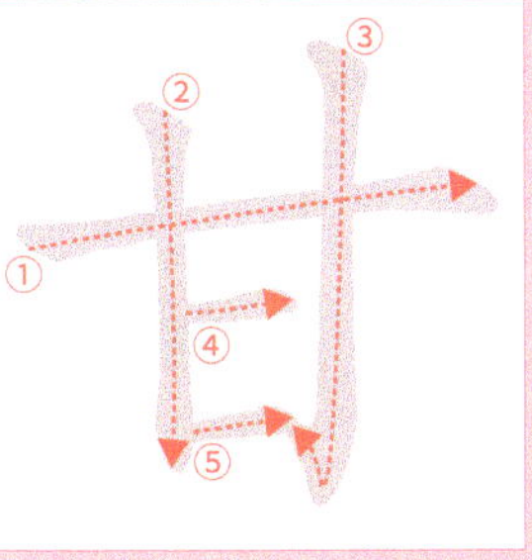 gān 甘 sweet (classical) | tián 甜 sweet | shèn 甚 extremely |
| 歹 evil | 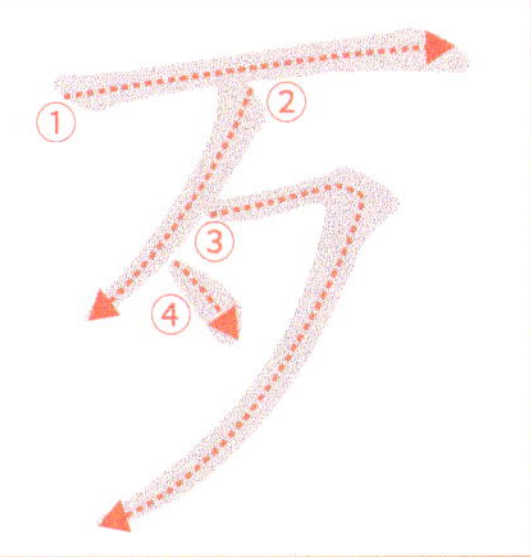 dǎi 歹 evil | sǐ 死 death | cán 残 cruel |

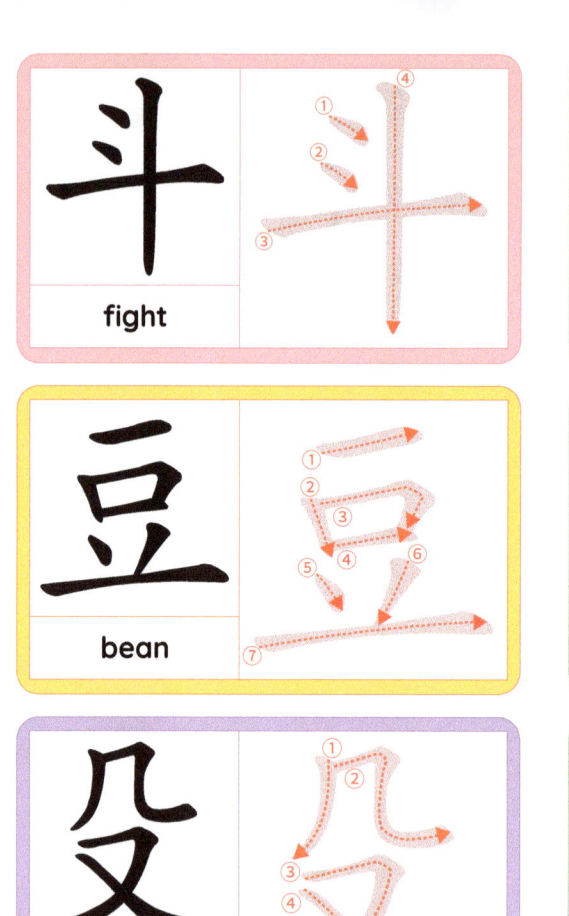

| | dòu | liào | zhēn |
|---|---|---|---|
| | 斗 fight | 料 material | 甚 to pour |
| | dòu | chǐ | wān |
| | 豆 bean | 豉 fermented beans | 豌 pea |
| | duàn | ōu | diàn |
| | 段 segment | 殴 beat | 殿 palace |
| | xīn | là | cí |
| | 辛 bitter | 辣 spicy | 辞 resign |
| | máo | tǎn | háo |
| | 毛 fur | 毯 blanket | 毫 tiny |
| | wéi | hán | rèn |
| | 韦 leather | 韩 Korea | 韧 tough |

— 21 —

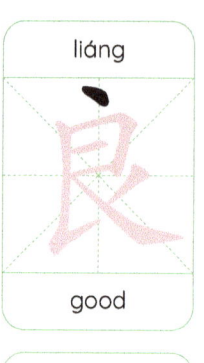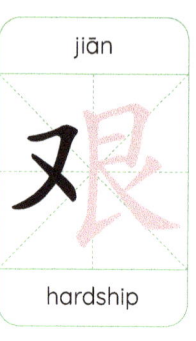

| | gèn | liáng | jiān |
|---|---|---|---|
| tough | tough | good | hardship |

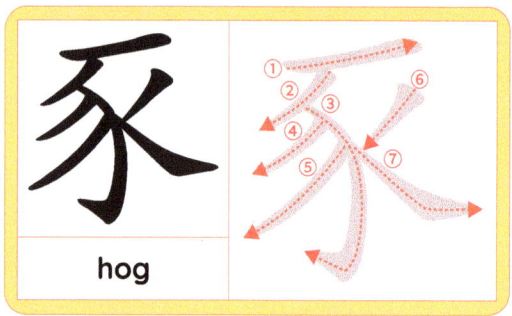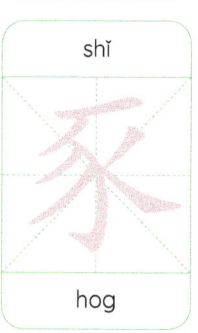

| | shǐ | xiàng | háo |
|---|---|---|---|
| hog | hog | elephant | magnificent |

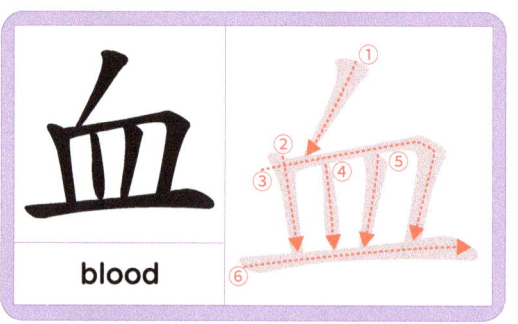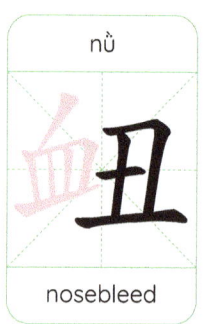

| | xuè | xìn | nǜ |
|---|---|---|---|
| blood | blood | grudge | nosebleed |

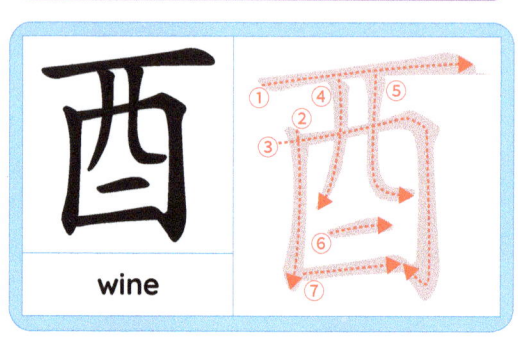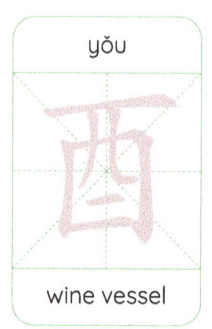

| | yǒu | zuì | chóu |
|---|---|---|---|
| wine | wine vessel | drunk | reward |

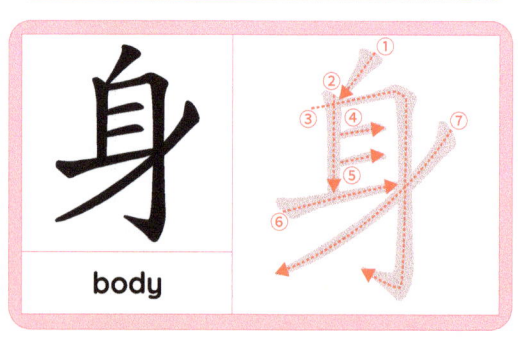

| | shēn | qū | duǒ |
|---|---|---|---|
| body | body | human body | to hide |

| | guǐ | mèi | pò |
|---|---|---|---|
| ghost | ghost | demon | spirit |

# CHINESE CHARACTERS

## YOUR NEXT 100 CHINESE CHARACTERS

It's time to take the next step again and learn your third set of 100 characters!

If you've completed Worbook 1 and 2, then you already know what to do. Start by tracing each character to build up that muscle memory, then challenge yourself to write each character on your own. For every character, you'll find three lines to trace and practice writing, and one final line to write freely without tracing. You've got this—I believe in you!

Mistakes are part of the journey, so don't worry if they happen. With practice, your writing will improve, and your confidence will grow. Most importantly, there's no need to rush, take your time and enjoy the process and have fun discovering the artistic side of Chinese characters! Don't forget to check out the example words for each character as well, this will really help supercharge your learning.

加油!
You can do it!

Need more space to practice?

# GIVING AND TAKING

**EXAMPLES**

买家 mǎi jiā buyer
买笔 mǎi bǐ to buy a pen
买东西 mǎi dōng xi to buy things

Radical: 一  Strokes: 6

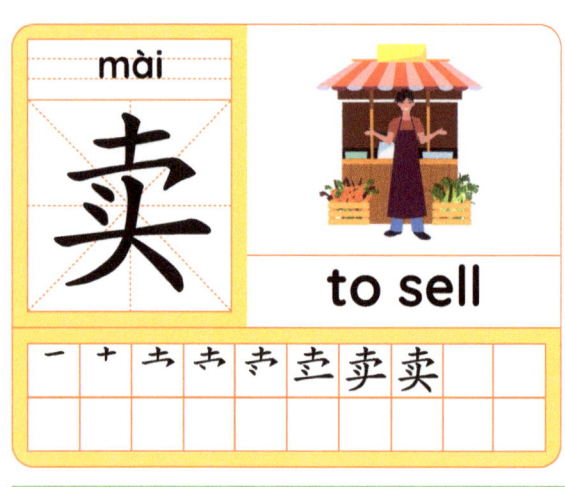

**EXAMPLES**

卖家 mài jiā seller
卖笔 mài bǐ to sell a pen
卖东西 mài dōng xi to sell things

Radical: 十  Strokes: 8

# GIVING AND TAKING

EXAMPLES

| 给我 | gěi wǒ | give to me |
| 给钱 | gěi qián | to give money |
| 给不给 | gěi bu gěi | to give or not |

Radical: 纟  Strokes: 9

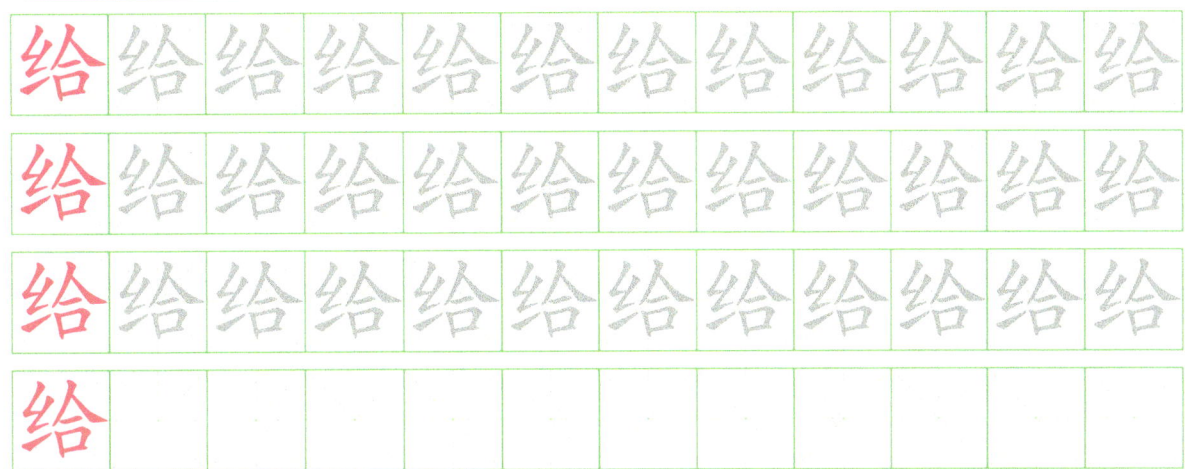

EXAMPLES

| 送礼 | sòng lǐ | to gift |
| 送钱 | sòng qián | to gift money |
| 送不送 | sòng bu sòng | to gift or not |

Radical: 辶  Strokes: 9

— 25 —

# GIVING AND TAKING

**ná** 拿 to take

丿 人 人 个 合 合 拿 拿 拿 拿

**EXAMPLES**

| 拿走 | ná zǒu | to take away |
| 拿药 | ná yào | to take away medicine |
| 拿货 | ná huò | to take goods |

Radical: 手    Strokes: 10

**rēng** 扔 to throw

一 扌 扌 扔 扔

**EXAMPLES**

| 扔了 | rēng le | threw away |
| 没扔 | méi rēng | didn't throw away |
| 别扔 | bié rēng | don't throw away |

Radical: 扌    Strokes: 5

# REQUESTS AND PERMISSIONS

**qǐng** — to invite; please

**EXAMPLES**

| 请问 | qǐng wèn | excuse me; may I ask |
| 请求 | qǐng qiú | to request |
| 请假 | qǐng jià | to ask for leave |

Radical: 讠　　Strokes: 10

**ràng** — to let; to make

**EXAMPLES**

| 让路 | ràng lù | to give way |
| 让座 | ràng zuò | to offer one's seat |
| 让步 | ràng bù | to give in |

Radical: 讠　　Strokes: 5

# REQUESTS AND PERMISSIONS

EXAMPLES

| 可以 | kě yǐ | yes; can do |
| 可是 | kě shì | however |
| 可能 | kě néng | maybe |

Radical: 口   Strokes: 5

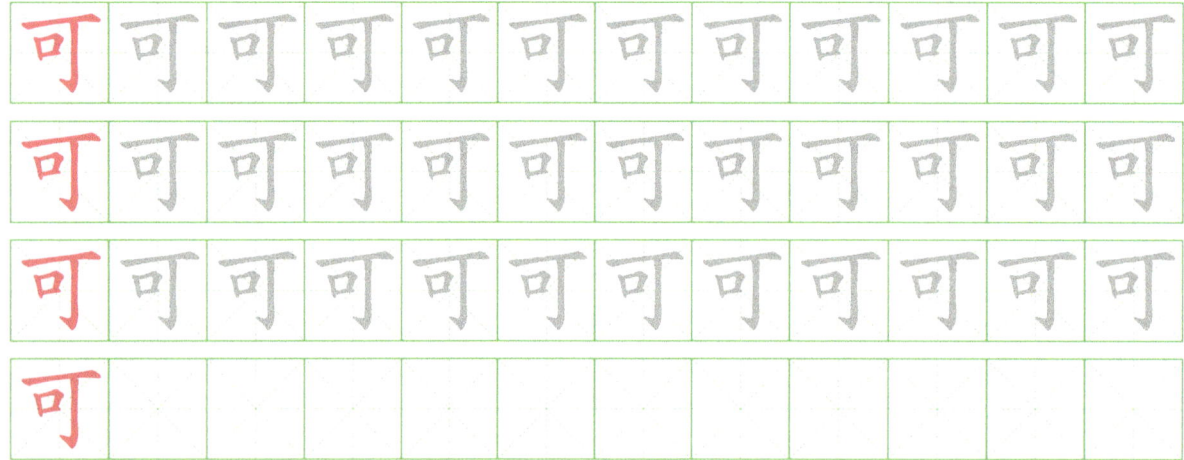

EXAMPLES

| 可否 | kě fǒu | yes or no |
| 否认 | fǒu rèn | to deny |
| 否则 | fǒu zé | otherwise |

Radical: 口   Strokes: 7

— 28 —

## REQUESTS AND PERMISSIONS

**EXAMPLES**

| 问答 | wèn dá | question and answer |
| 回答 | huí dá | to answer |
| 答案 | dá àn | answer |

Radical: 竹　　Strokes: 12

**EXAMPLES**

| 车把 | chē bǎ | handlebar |
| 火把 | huǒ bǎ | fire torch |
| 门把 | mén bǎ | door handle |

Radical: 扌　　Strokes: 7

# THINKING AND ABILITY

**EXAMPLES**

| 想吃 | xiǎng chī | want to eat |
| 想喝 | xiǎng hē | want to drink |
| 想家 | xiǎng jiā | to miss home |

Radical: 心   Strokes: 13

**EXAMPLES**

| 要去 | yào qù | want to go |
| 要走 | yào zǒu | intend to leave |
| 要留 | yào liú | intend to stay |

Radical: 西   Strokes: 9

# THINKING AND ABILITY

**EXAMPLES**

| 知道 | zhī dào | to know (aware) |
| 知名 | zhī míng | famous |
| 知识 | zhī shi | knowledge |

Radical: 矢    Strokes: 8

**EXAMPLES**

| 认识 | rèn shi | to know (person) |
| 识字 | shí zì | to be literate |
| 见识 | jiàn shi | insight |

Radical: 讠    Strokes: 7

— 31 —

# THINKING AND ABILITY

huì
会
can; will

丿 人 人 会 会 会

**EXAMPLES**

| 会说 | huì shuō | can speak |
| 会读 | huì dú | can read |
| 会写 | huì xiě | can write |

Radical: 人    Strokes: 6

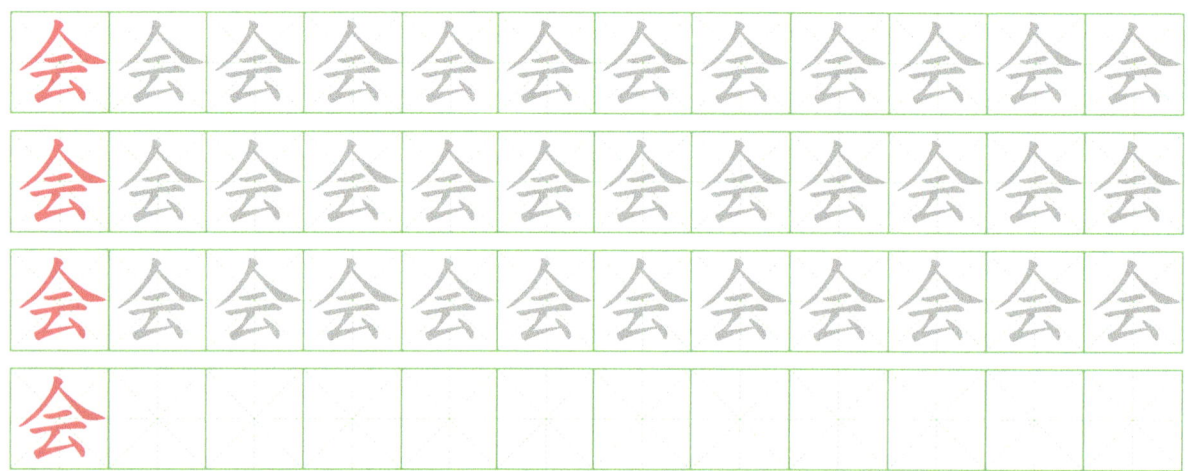

néng
能
be able to

㔾 厶 ㄅ 台 自 自 能 能 能

**EXAMPLES**

| 能做 | néng zuò | able to do |
| 能唱 | néng chàng | able to sing |
| 能跳 | néng tiào | able to dance |

Radical: 月    Strokes: 10

# EMOTIONS AND FEELINGS

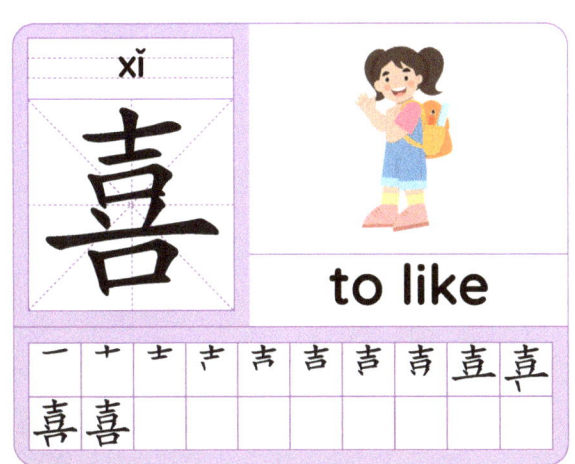

EXAMPLES

| 喜欢 | xǐ huān | to like |
| 喜爱 | xǐ ài | to adore |
| 喜剧 | xǐ jù | comedy |

Radical: 口   Strokes: 12

EXAMPLES

| 讨厌 | tǎo yàn | to dislike |
| 厌烦 | yàn fán | be fed up with |
| 厌食 | yàn shí | to lack appetite |

Radical: 厂   Strokes: 6

# EMOTIONS AND FEELINGS

**ài** — 爱 — to love

EXAMPLES

| 爱好 | ài hào | hobby |
| 爱人 | ài rén | spouse |
| 爱情 | ài qíng | love (romance) |

Radical: 爫   Strokes: 10

**hèn** — 恨 — to hate

EXAMPLES

| 仇恨 | chóu hèn | hatred |
| 恨谁 | hèn shéi | hate who? |
| 爱恨 | ài hèn | love and hate |

Radical: 忄   Strokes: 9

# EMOTIONS AND FEELINGS

**kū** — 哭 — to cry

Strokes: 丨 口 口 吅 吅 吅 吅 哭 哭

**EXAMPLES**

| 大哭 | dà kū | cry loudly |
| 别哭 | bié kū | don't cry |
| 哭脸 | kū liǎn | crying face |

Radical: 口    Strokes: 10

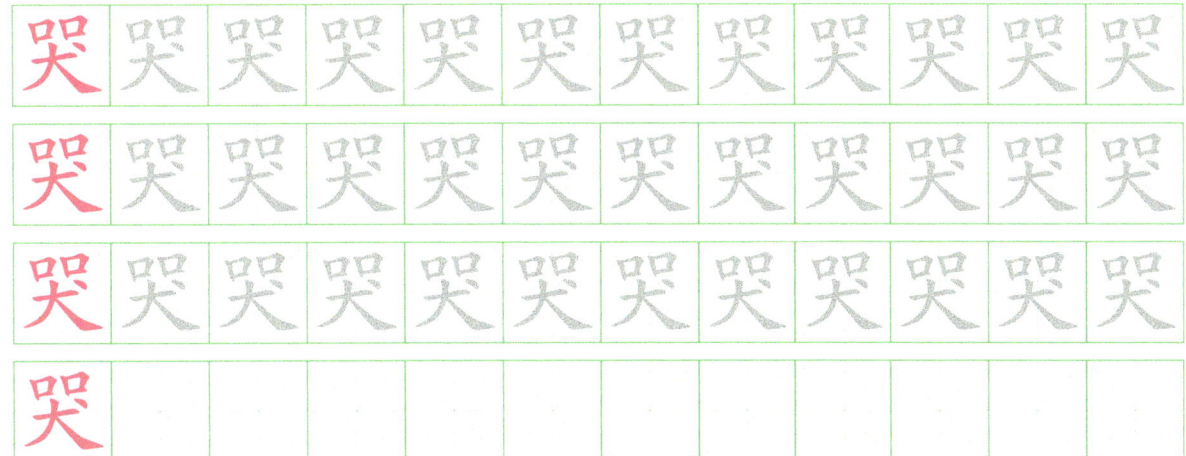

**xiào** — 笑 — to laugh

Strokes: 丿 𠂉 𠂉 𠂉 竹 竹 竺 竺 笋 笑

**EXAMPLES**

| 大笑 | dà xiào | laugh loudly |
| 别笑 | bié xiào | don't laugh |
| 笑脸 | xiào liǎn | laughing face |

Radical: 竹    Strokes: 10

# EMOTIONS AND FEELINGS

**lè** — to cheer

Stroke order: 丿 ⺁ 乐 乐 乐

EXAMPLES

| 快乐 | kuài lè | happy |
| 欢乐 | huān lè | joy |
| 乐什么 | lè shén me | cheer for what? |

Radical: 丿   Strokes: 5

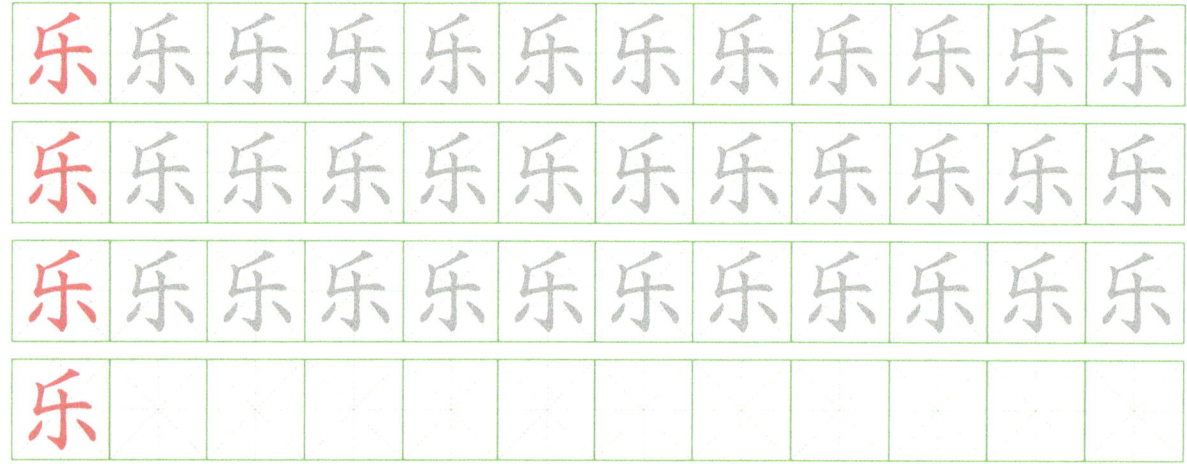

**qì** — to be angry; air

Stroke order: 丿 ⺁ 匚 气

EXAMPLES

| 生气 | shēng qì | angry |
| 空气 | kōng qì | air |
| 气什么 | qì shén me | angry about what? |

Radical: 气   Strokes: 4

# BODY PARTS

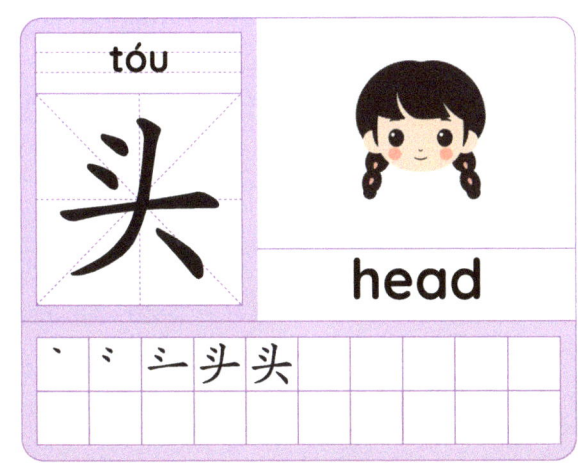

**EXAMPLES**

| 头发 | tóu fa | hair |
| 头痛 | tóu tòng | headache |
| 抬头 | tái tóu | to look up |

Radical: 大    Strokes: 5

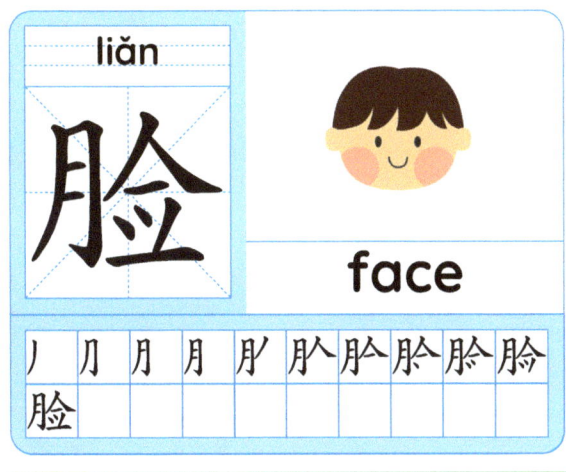

**EXAMPLES**

| 圆脸 | yuán liǎn | round face |
| 丢脸 | diū liǎn | to lose face |
| 脸红 | liǎn hóng | to blush |

Radical: 月    Strokes: 11

# BODY PARTS

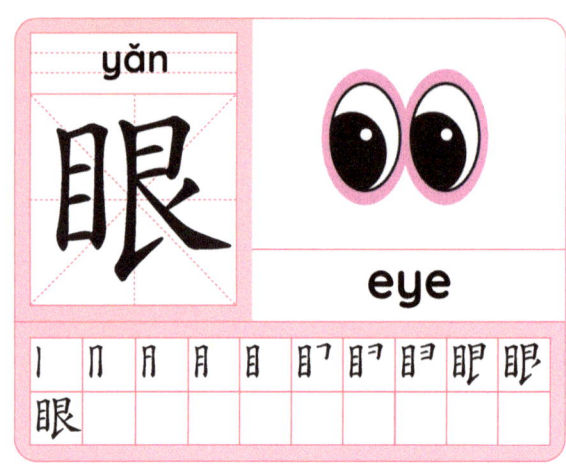

EXAMPLES

| 眼睛 | yǎn jīng | eyes |
| 眼镜 | yǎn jìng | glasses |
| 眼球 | yǎn qiú | eyeballs |

Radical: 目    Strokes: 11

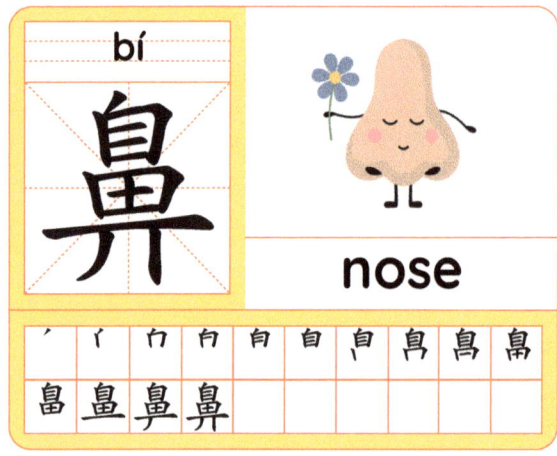

EXAMPLES

| 鼻子 | bí zi | nose |
| 鼻血 | bí xuè | nosebleed |
| 鼻尖 | bí jiān | tip of nose |

Radical: 鼻    Strokes: 14

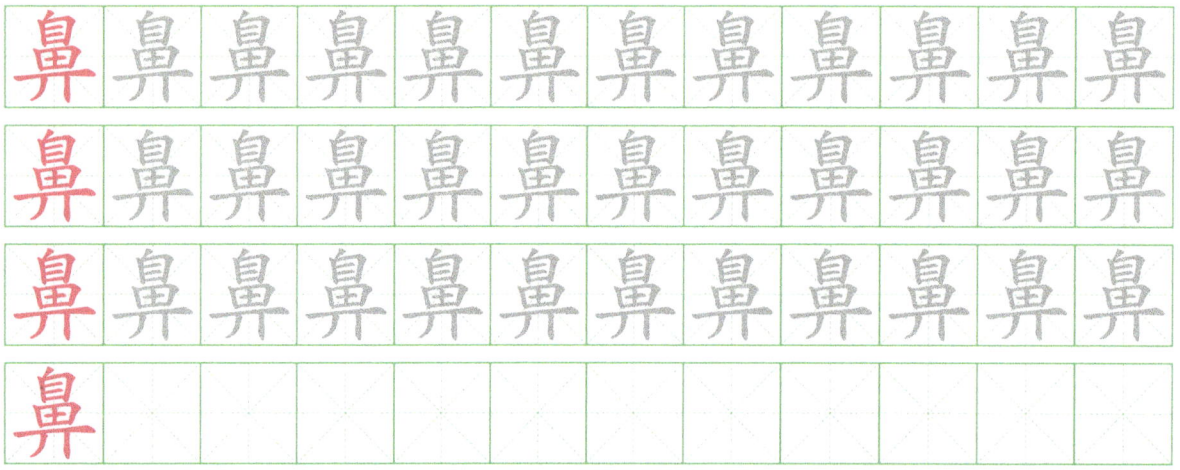

— 38 —

# BODY PARTS

EXAMPLES

| 嘴巴 | zuǐ ba | mouth |
| 张嘴 | zhāng zuǐ | to open mouth |
| 闭嘴 | bì zuǐ | to shut up |

Radical: 口   Strokes: 16

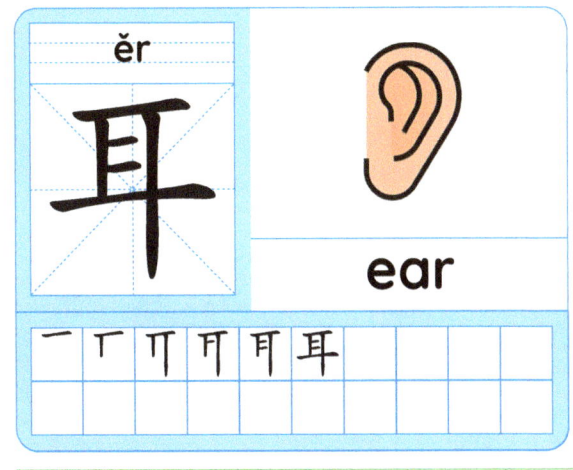

EXAMPLES

| 耳朵 | ěr duo | ear |
| 左耳 | zuǒ ěr | left ear |
| 右耳 | yòu ěr | right ear |

Radical: 耳   Strokes: 6

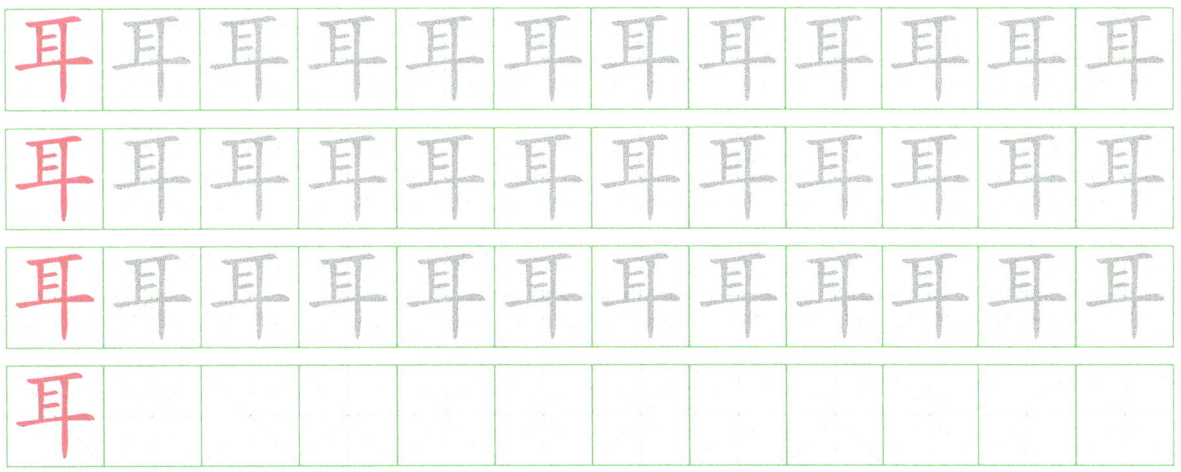

# BODY PARTS

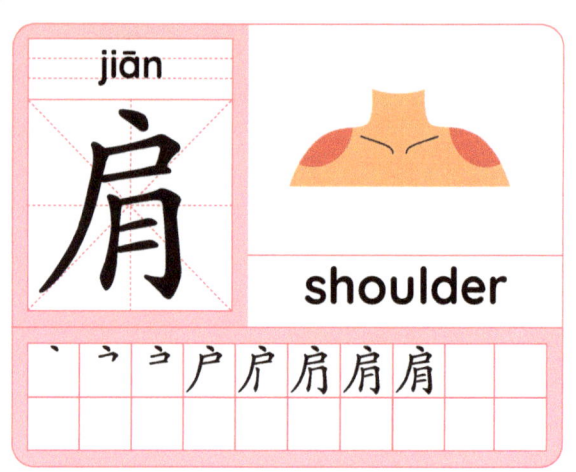

jiān
肩
shoulder
丶 ㇉ ㇌ 户 户 肩 肩 肩

EXAMPLES

肩膀   jiān bǎng   shoulder
左肩   zuǒ jiān   left shoulder
右肩   yòu jiān   right shoulder

Radical: 月   Strokes: 8

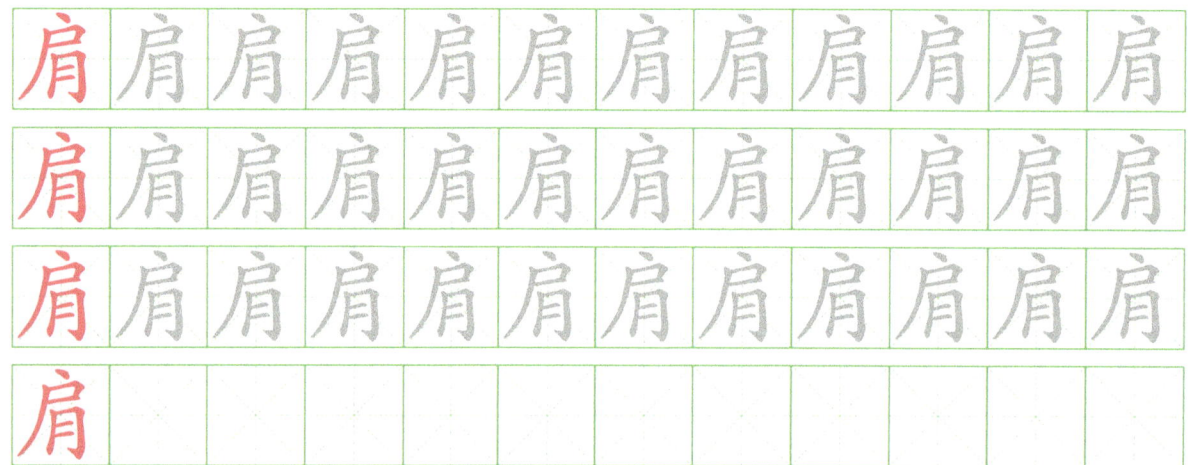

shǒu
手
hand
一 二 三 手

EXAMPLES

手臂   shǒu bì    arm
手机   shǒu jī    mobile phone
手术   shǒu shù   surgery

Radical: 手   Strokes: 4

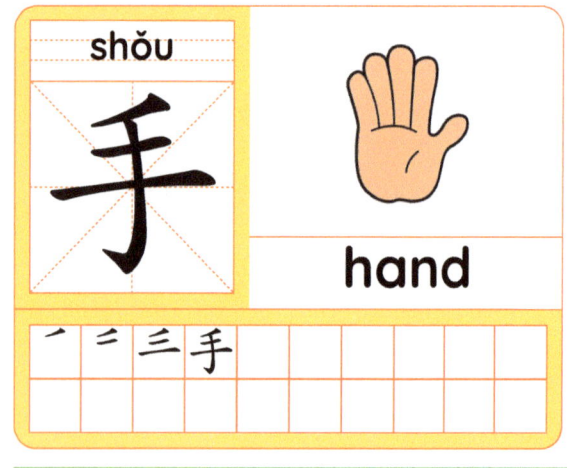

# BODY PARTS

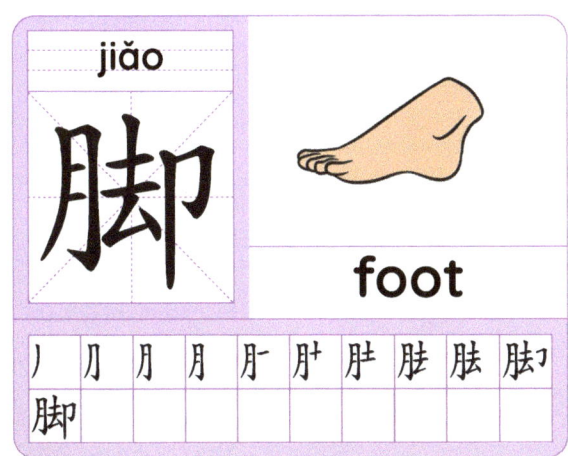

jiǎo
脚
foot

丿 刂 月 月 肝 肝 肝 肚 胠 脚

**EXAMPLES**

| 脚趾 | jiǎo zhǐ | toe |
| 左脚 | zuǒ jiǎo | left foot |
| 右脚 | yòu jiǎo | right foot |

Radical: 月　　Strokes: 11

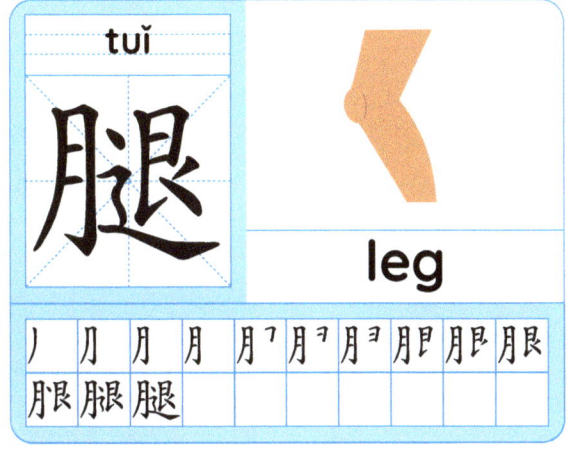

tuǐ
腿
leg

丿 刂 月 月 月⁷ 月ㄋ 月ㅋ 肝 胆 胆 腿 腿 腿

**EXAMPLES**

| 火腿 | huǒ tuǐ | ham |
| 左腿 | zuǒ tuǐ | left leg |
| 右腿 | yòu tuǐ | right leg |

Radical: 月　　Strokes: 13

# BODY PARTS

**EXAMPLES**

| | | |
|---|---|---|
| 心脏 | xīn zàng | heart (medical term) |
| 开心 | kāi xīn | happy |
| 伤心 | shāng xīn | sad |

Radical: 心    Strokes: 4

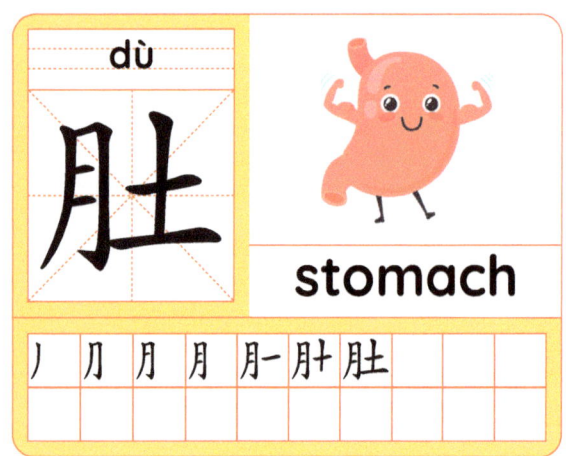

**EXAMPLES**

| | | |
|---|---|---|
| 肚子 | dù zi | stomach |
| 肚里 | dù lǐ | in the stomach |
| 肚皮 | dù pí | belly |

Radical: 月    Strokes: 7

— 42 —

# PERSONAL BELONGINGS

**shū** — book

一 乛 书 书

EXAMPLES

| 书桌 | shū zhuō | desk |
| 书店 | shū diàn | bookstore |
| 一本书 | yì běn shū | a book |

Radical: 一　　Strokes: 4

**běn** — notebook

一 十 才 木 本

EXAMPLES

| 本子 | běn zi | notebook |
| 画本 | huà běn | drawing book |
| 课本 | kè běn | textbook |

Radical: 木　　Strokes: 5

# PERSONAL BELONGINGS

EXAMPLES

| 书包 | shū bāo | school bag |
| 背包 | bēi bāo | backpack |
| 面包 | miàn bāo | bread |

Radical: 勹   Strokes: 5

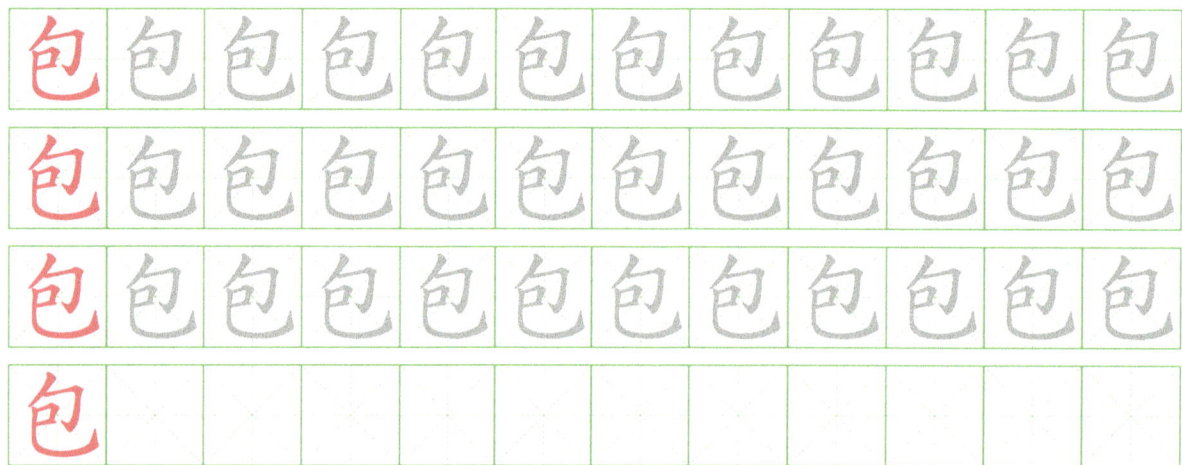

EXAMPLES

| 铅笔 | qiān bǐ | pencil |
| 钢笔 | gāng bǐ | fountain pen |
| 毛笔 | máo bǐ | brush pen |

Radical: 竹   Strokes: 10

— 44 —

# PERSONAL BELONGINGS

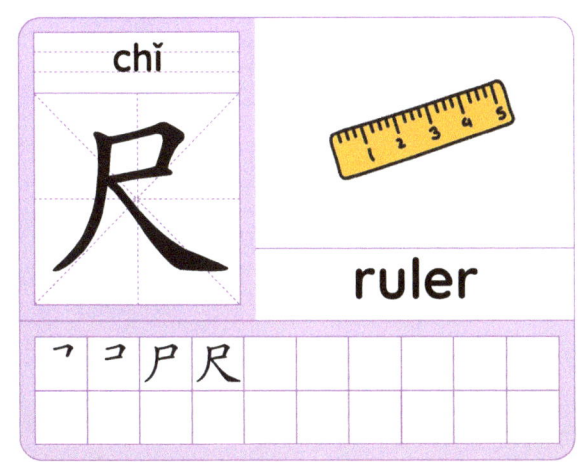

**EXAMPLES**

| 尺子 | chǐ zi | ruler |
| 尺寸 | chǐ cùn | size |
| 七尺 | qī chǐ | seven feet (measurement) |

Radical: 尸    Strokes: 4

**EXAMPLES**

| 纸条 | zhǐ tiáo | (paper) note |
| 纸巾 | zhǐ jīn | tissue paper |
| 一张纸 | yì zhāng zhǐ | a piece of paper |

Radical: 纟    Strokes: 7

— 45 —

# PERSONAL BELONGINGS

**EXAMPLES**

| 有钱 | yǒu qián | rich |
| 没钱 | méi qián | poor |
| 花钱 | huā qián | to spend money |

Radical: 钅  Strokes: 10

**EXAMPLES**

| 卡片 | kǎ piàn | greeting card |
| 卡号 | kǎ hào | card number |
| 卡通 | kǎ tōng | cartoon |

Radical: 卜  Strokes: 5

# PERSONAL BELONGINGS

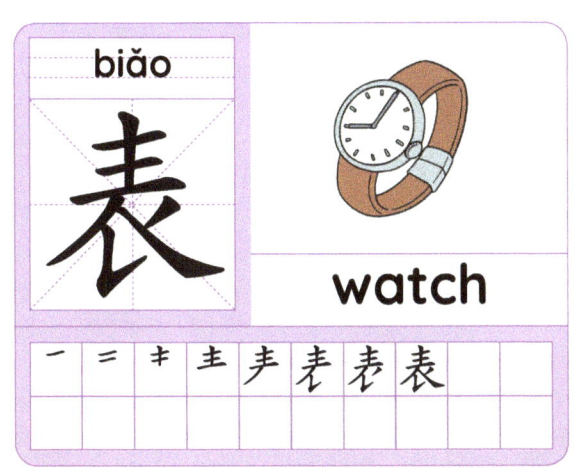

| | | EXAMPLES | |
|---|---|---|---|
| | 手表 | shǒu biǎo | watch |
| | 金表 | jīn biǎo | gold watch |
| | 银表 | yín biǎo | silver watch |

Radical: 衣    Strokes: 8

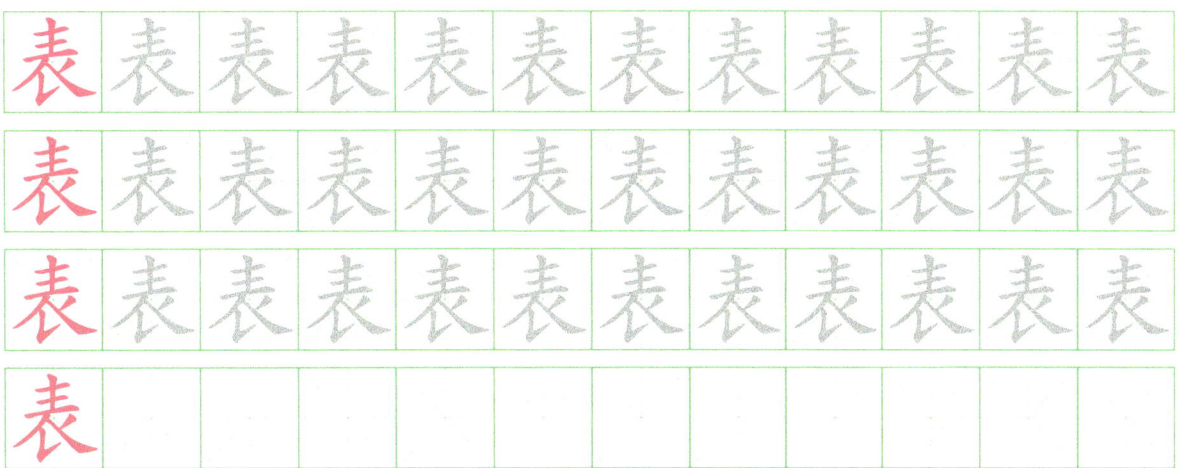

| | | EXAMPLES | |
|---|---|---|---|
| | 足球 | zú qiú | football |
| | 篮球 | lán qiú | basketball |
| | 网球 | wǎng qiú | tennis |

Radical: 王    Strokes: 11

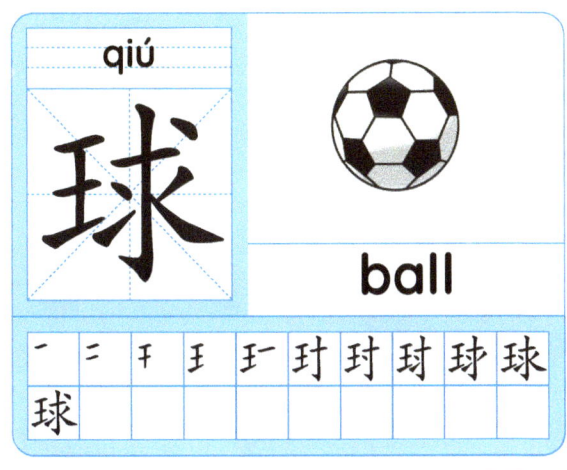

— 47 —

# TRANSPORTATION

**chē** — car; vehicle

一 七 车 车

Radical: 车　Strokes: 4

### EXAMPLES

| 火车 | huǒ chē | train |
| 汽车 | qì chē | car |
| 班车 | bān chē | bus |

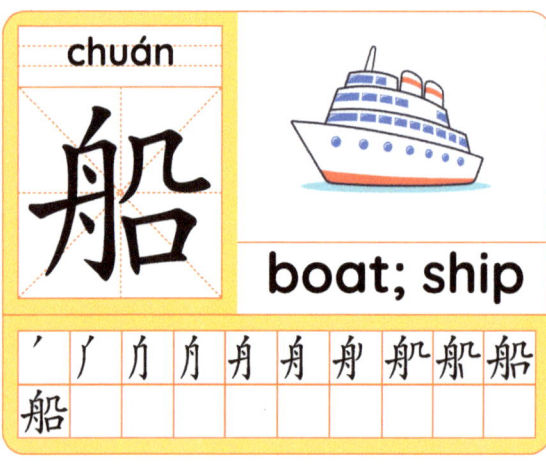

**chuán** — boat; ship

′ 丿 丿 凢 凢 舟 舟 舢 舩 船

Radical: 舟　Strokes: 11

### EXAMPLES

| 游船 | yóu chuán | cruise ship |
| 木船 | mù chuán | wooden boat |
| 飞船 | fēi chuán | spaceship |

# TRANSPORTATION

jī

机

aircraft; machine

一 十 才 木 朳 机

**EXAMPLES**

| 飞机 | fēi jī | airplane |
| 机器 | jī qì | machine |
| 机器人 | jī qì rén | robot |

Radical: 木     Strokes: 6

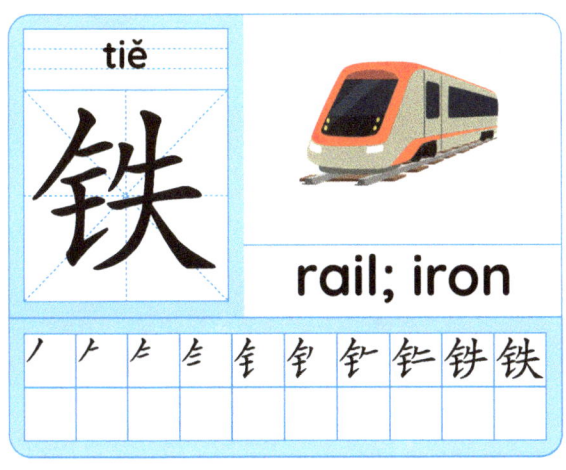

tiě

铁

rail; iron

丿 ㇒ ㇏ ㇉ 钅 钅 钅 铲 铗 铁

**EXAMPLES**

| 高铁 | gāo tiě | high-speed rail |
| 地铁 | dì tiě | subway |
| 铁锅 | tiě guō | iron pan |

Radical: 钅     Strokes: 10

# BUILDINGS AND ROOMS

**diàn** — shop

Stroke order: 丶 一 广 广 庐 店 店

### EXAMPLES

| 酒店 | jiǔ diàn | hotel |
| 商店 | shāng diàn | shop |
| 书店 | shū diàn | book shop |

Radical: 广   Strokes: 8

**guǎn** — place (services)

Stroke order: ノ 𠃋 饣 饣 饣 饣 饣 馆 馆

### EXAMPLES

| 饭馆 | fàn guǎn | restaurant |
| 茶馆 | chá guǎn | tea house |
| 咖啡馆 | kā fēi guǎn | coffee shop |

Radical: 饣   Strokes: 11

— 50 —

# BUILDINGS AND ROOMS

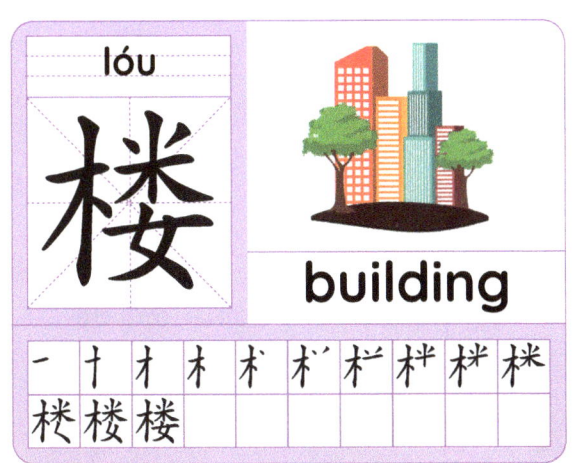

**EXAMPLES**

| 楼房 | lóu fáng | building |
| 上楼 | shàng lóu | to go upstairs |
| 下楼 | xià lóu | to go downstairs |

Radical: 木   Strokes: 13

**EXAMPLES**

| 房子 | fáng zi | house |
| 书房 | shū fáng | study room |
| 房东 | fáng dōng | landlord |

Radical: 户   Strokes: 8

# BUILDINGS AND ROOMS

## jiān — 间 — room; space

Stroke order: 丶 冂 门 门 问 间 间

**EXAMPLES**

| 房间 | fáng jiān | room (of a house) |
| 时间 | shí jiān | time |
| 课间 | kè jiān | break between classes |

Radical: 门   Strokes: 7

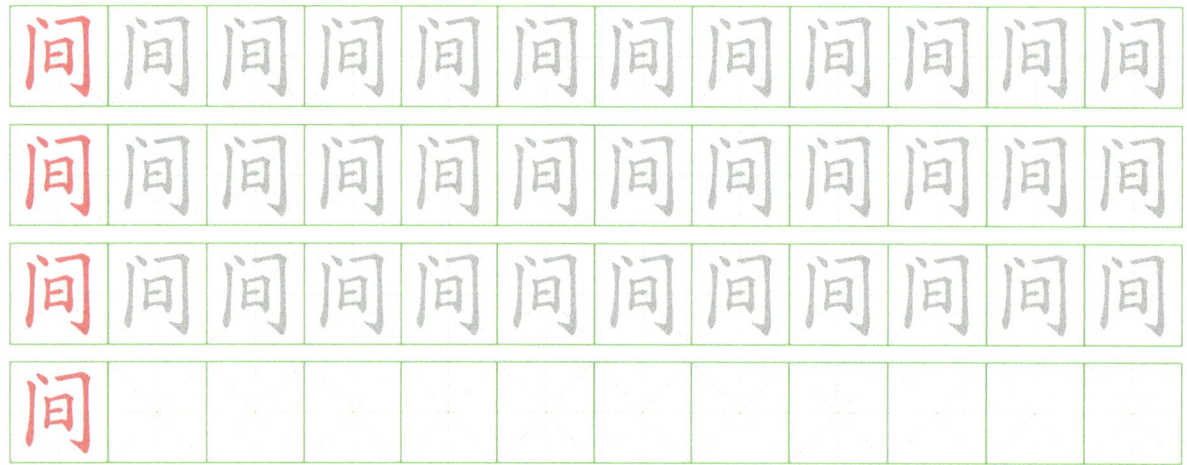

## shì — 室 — room; place

Stroke order: 丶 丶 宀 宁 宀 宫 室 室 室

**EXAMPLES**

| 卧室 | wò shì | bedroom |
| 教室 | jiào shì | classroom |
| 室友 | shì yǒu | roommate |

Radical: 宀   Strokes: 9

# PLACES

| | | |
|---|---|---|
| 国家 | guó jiā | nation; country |
| 国内 | guó nèi | domestic |
| 国外 | guó wài | abroad |

EXAMPLES

Radical: 囗   Strokes: 8

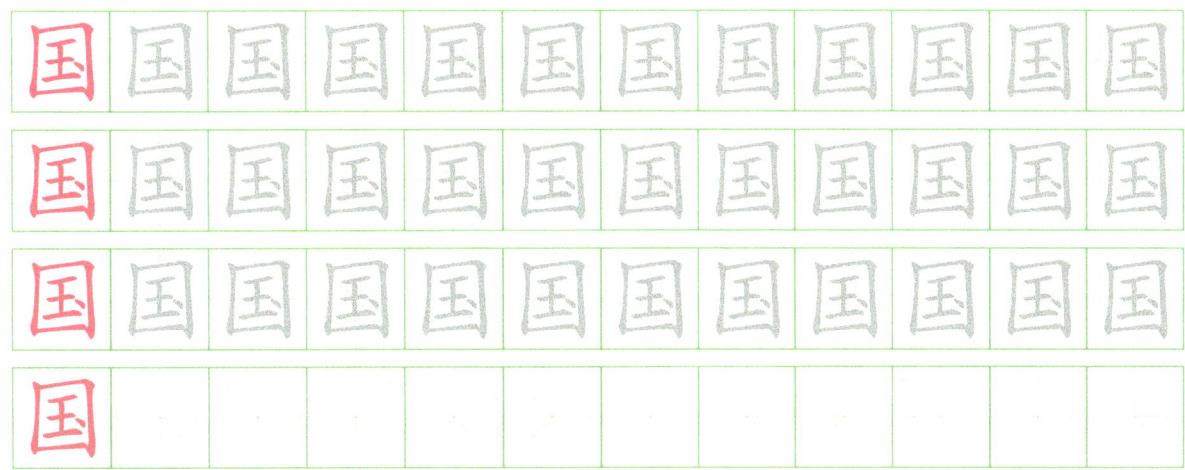

EXAMPLES

| | | |
|---|---|---|
| 家人 | jiā rén | family member |
| 回家 | huí jiā | to go home |
| 大家 | dà jiā | everyone |

Radical: 宀   Strokes: 10

# PLACES

| EXAMPLES | | |
|---|---|---|
| 城市 | chéng shì | city |
| 市场 | shì chǎng | market |
| 市中心 | shì zhōng xīn | city center |

Radical: 巾   Strokes: 5

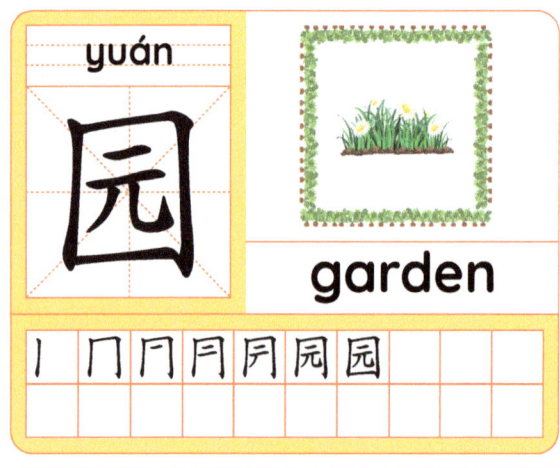

| EXAMPLES | | |
|---|---|---|
| 花园 | huā yuán | garden (flower) |
| 菜园 | cài yuán | vegetable garden |
| 公园 | gōng yuán | park |

Radical: 囗   Strokes: 7

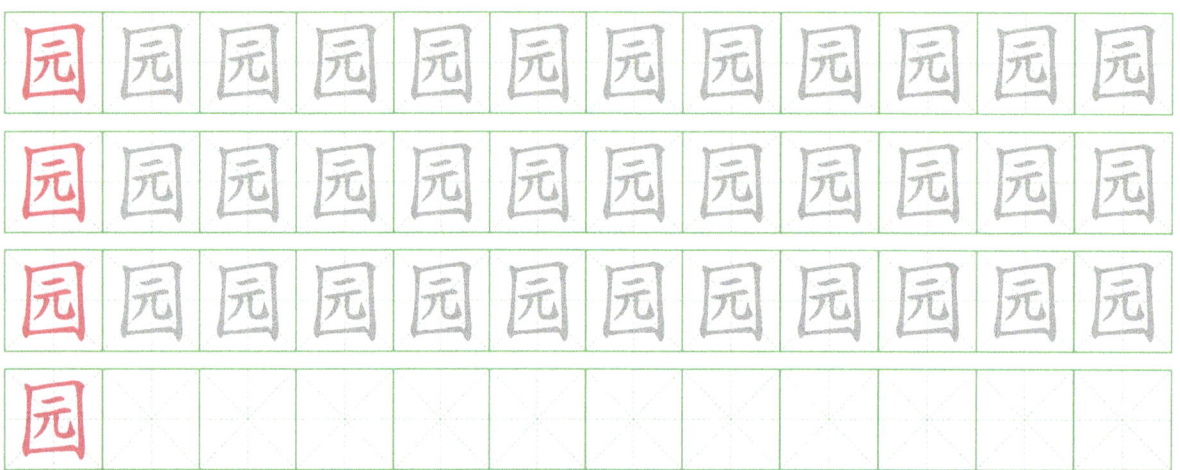

# PLACES

**EXAMPLES**

| 公路 | gōng lù | highway |
| 铁路 | tiě lù | railway |
| 路口 | lù kǒu | intersection |

Radical: 足  Strokes: 13

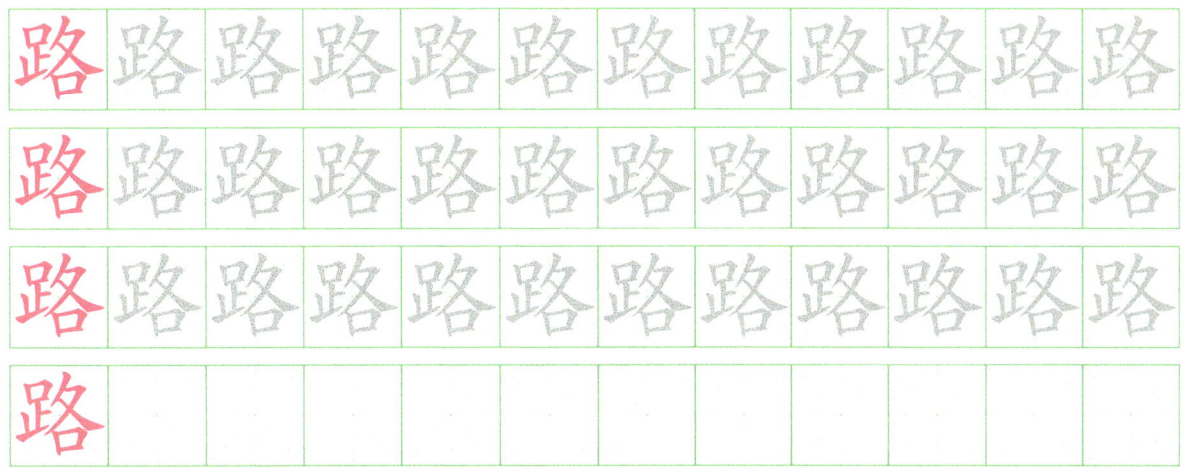

**EXAMPLES**

| 街道 | jiē dào | street |
| 街上 | jiē shàng | on the street |
| 逛街 | guàng jiē | go shopping |

Radical: 彳  Strokes: 12

# PLACES

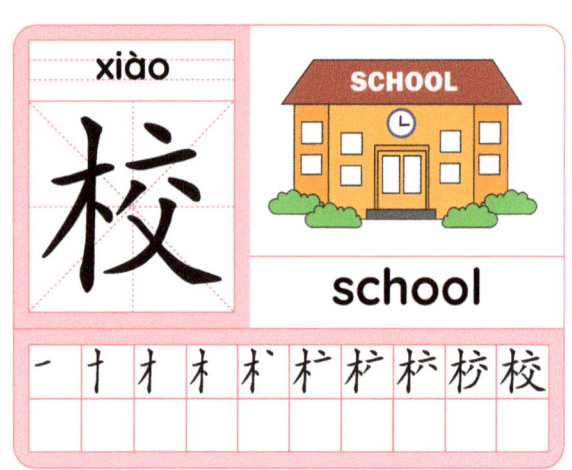

**EXAMPLES**

| 学校 | xué xiào | school |
| 校长 | xiào zhǎng | principal (school) |
| 校园 | xiào yuán | campus |

Radical: 木    Strokes: 10

**EXAMPLES**

| 学院 | xué yuàn | college department |
| 院长 | yuàn zhǎng | dean |
| 院子 | yuàn zi | yard; court |

Radical: 阝    Strokes: 9

# TABLEWARE

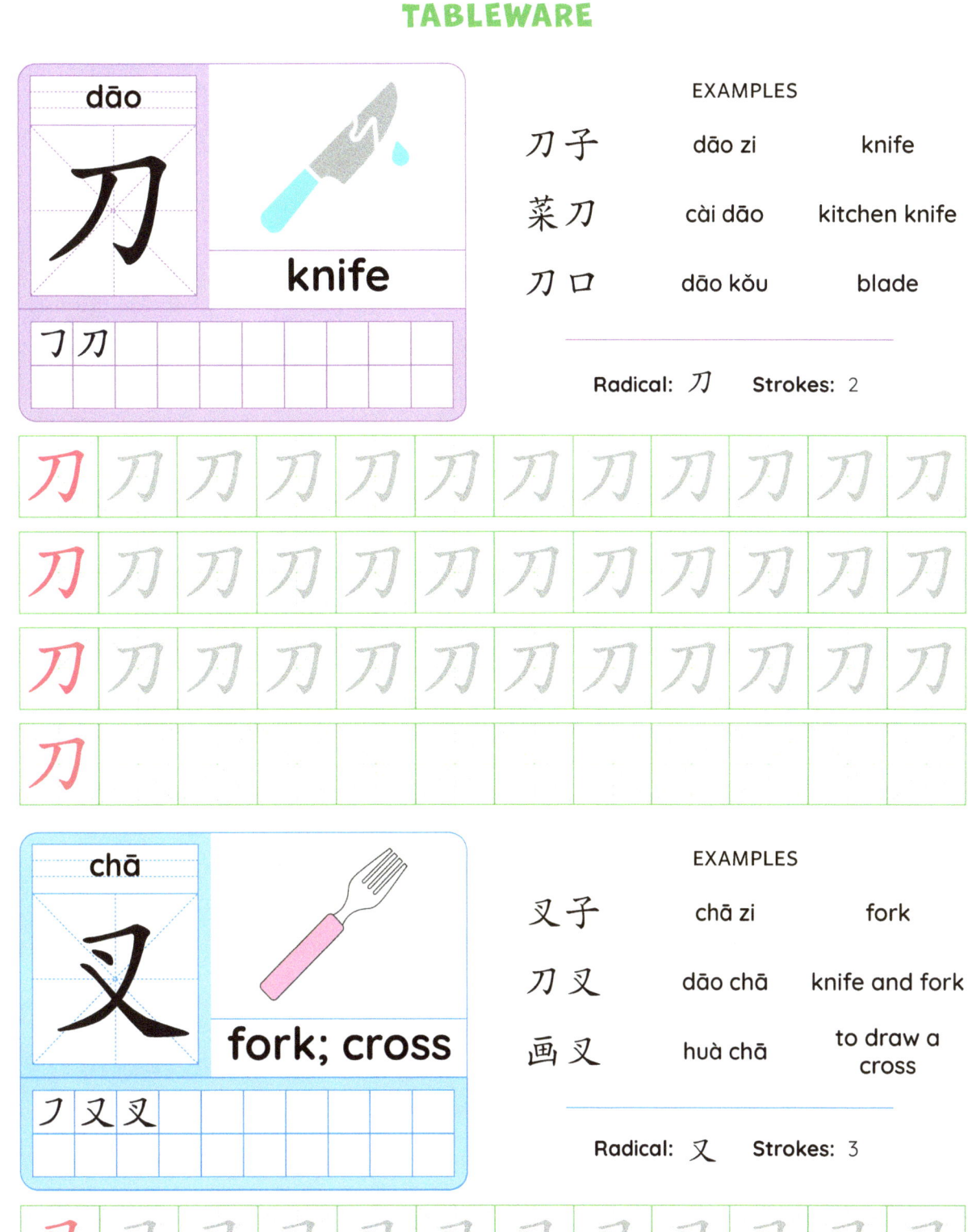

**dāo** — 刀 — knife

笔顺: 丁 刀

EXAMPLES

| 刀子 | dāo zi | knife |
| 菜刀 | cài dāo | kitchen knife |
| 刀口 | dāo kǒu | blade |

Radical: 刀    Strokes: 2

**chā** — 叉 — fork; cross

笔顺: 丁 又 叉

EXAMPLES

| 叉子 | chā zi | fork |
| 刀叉 | dāo chā | knife and fork |
| 画叉 | huà chā | to draw a cross |

Radical: 又    Strokes: 3

# TABLEWARE

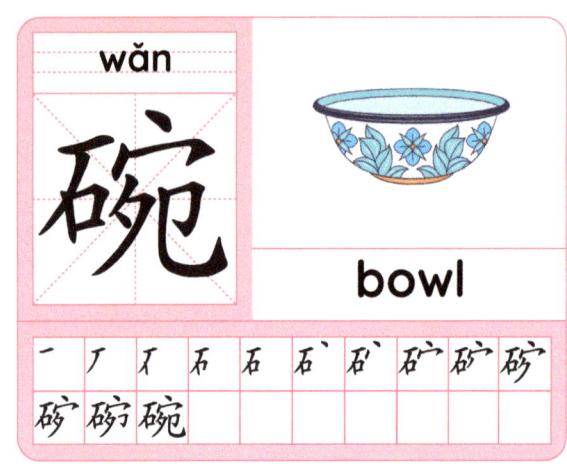

**wǎn** — 碗 — bowl

### EXAMPLES

| 小碗 | xiǎo wǎn | small bowl |
| 大碗 | dà wǎn | big bowl |
| 碗柜 | wǎn guì | cupboard (cutlery) |

Radical: 石    Strokes: 13

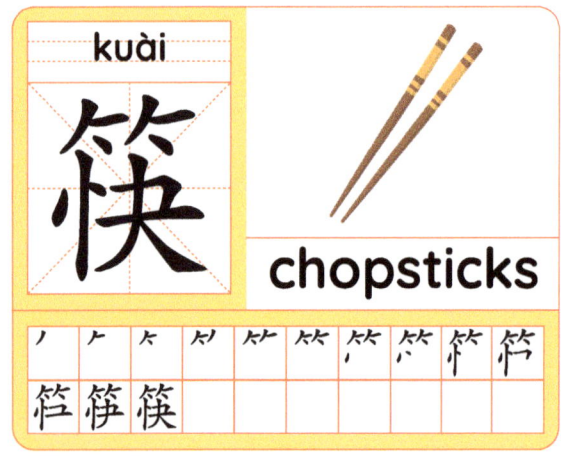

**kuài** — 筷 — chopsticks

### EXAMPLES

| 筷子 | kuài zi | chopsticks |
| 碗筷 | wǎn kuài | bowls and chopsticks |
| 木筷 | mù kuài | wooden chopsticks |

Radical: 竹    Strokes: 13

# TABLEWARE

**EXAMPLES**

| 盘子 | pán zi | plate |
| 键盘 | jiàn pán | keyboard |
| 算盘 | suàn pán | abacus |

Radical: 皿  Strokes: 11

**EXAMPLES**

| 勺子 | sháo zi | spoon |
| 汤勺 | tāng sháo | soup spoon |
| 饭勺 | fàn sháo | rice spoon |

Radical: 勺  Strokes: 3

# TABLEWARE

**bēi** — cup; glass

一 十 才 才 木 朳 杯 杯

**EXAMPLES**

| 杯子 | bēi zi | cup |
| 酒杯 | jiǔ bēi | wine glass |
| 一杯茶 | yì bēi chá | a cup of tea |

Radical: 木    Strokes: 8

**píng** — bottle

丶 丷 䒑 兰 羊 并 并 瓶 瓶 瓶

**EXAMPLES**

| 瓶子 | píng zi | bottle |
| 瓶盖 | píng gài | bottle cap |
| 一瓶水 | yì píng shuǐ | a bottle of water |

Radical: 瓦    Strokes: 10

# FOOD

**EXAMPLES**

| 米饭 | mǐ fàn | cooked rice |
| 米粉 | mǐ fěn | rice noodles |
| 米酒 | mǐ jiǔ | rice wine |

Radical: 米    Strokes: 6

**EXAMPLES**

| 早饭 | zǎo fàn | breakfast |
| 午饭 | wǔ fàn | lunch meal |
| 晚饭 | wǎn fàn | dinner |

Radical: 饣    Strokes: 7

# FOOD

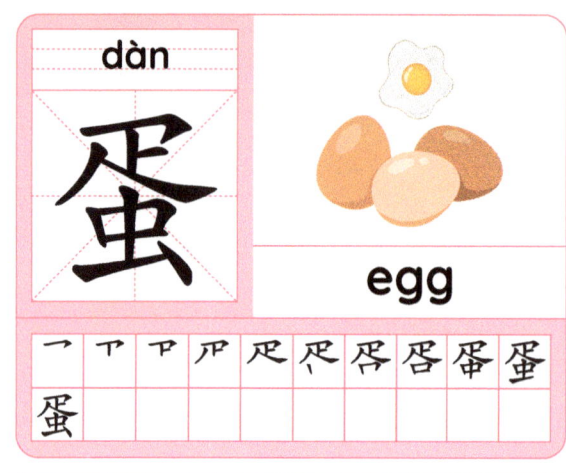

**EXAMPLES**

| 鸡蛋 | jī dàn | chicken egg |
| 鸭蛋 | yā dàn | duck egg |
| 下蛋 | xià dàn | to lay an egg |

Radical: 虫　　Strokes: 11

**EXAMPLES**

| 猪肉 | zhū ròu | pork |
| 牛肉 | niú ròu | beef |
| 鸡肉 | jī ròu | chicken |

Radical: 冂　　Strokes: 6

# FOOD

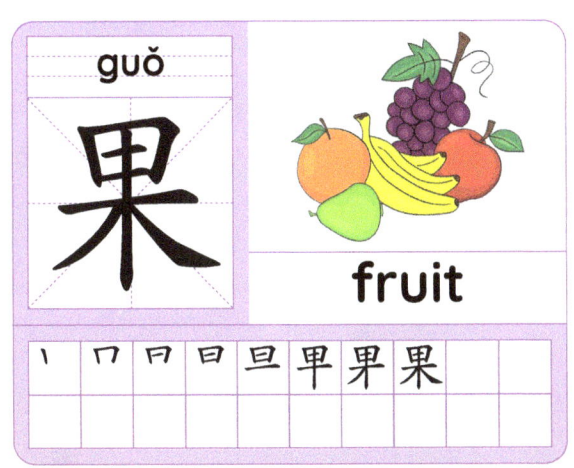

| EXAMPLES | | |
|---|---|---|
| 水果 | shuǐ guǒ | fruit |
| 苹果 | píng guǒ | apple |
| 芒果 | máng guǒ | mango |

Radical: 木　Strokes: 8

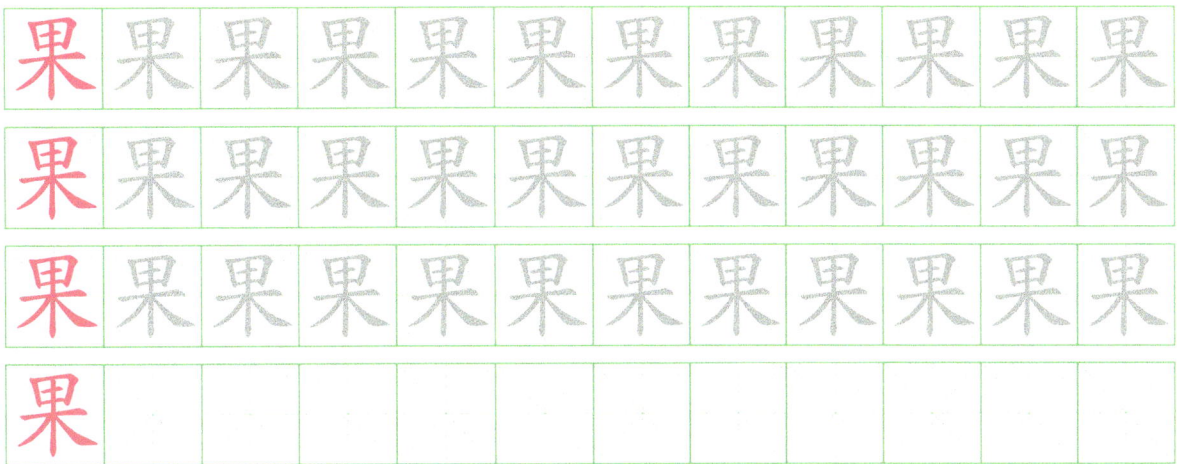

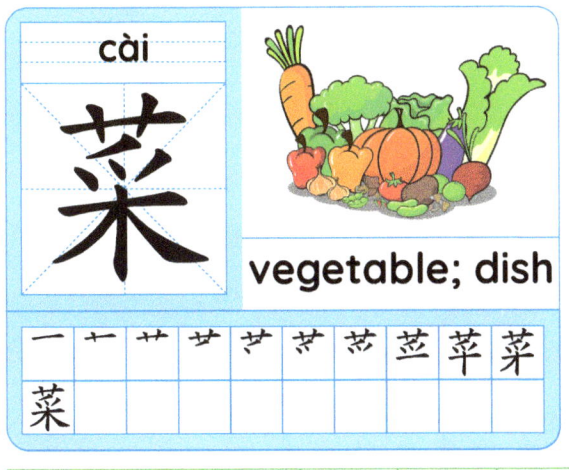

| EXAMPLES | | |
|---|---|---|
| 蔬菜 | shū cài | vegetable |
| 做菜 | zuò cài | to cook dishes |
| 菜单 | cài dān | menu |

Radical: 艹　Strokes: 11

# FOOD

**miàn** — flour; noodle

一 ナ 广 丙 而 而 面 面

**EXAMPLES**

| 面粉 | miàn fěn | flour |
| 面团 | miàn tuán | dough |
| 面条 | miàn tiáo | noodles |

Radical: 面   Strokes: 9

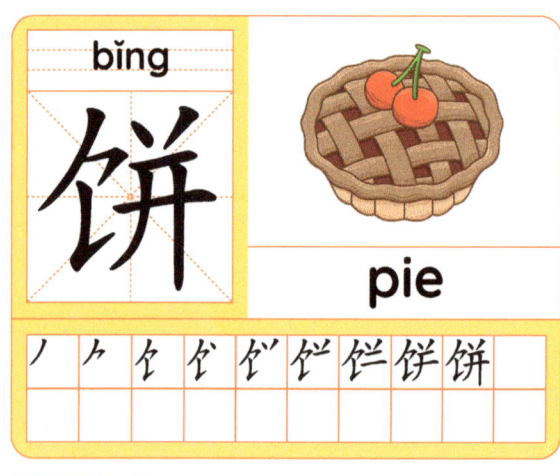

**bǐng** — pie

丿 乂 乆 乆 饣 饣 饼 饼 饼

**EXAMPLES**

| 饼子 | bǐng zi | pie |
| 饼干 | bǐng gān | cookie; cracker |
| 月饼 | yuè bǐng | mooncake |

Radical: 饣   Strokes: 9

# DRINKS

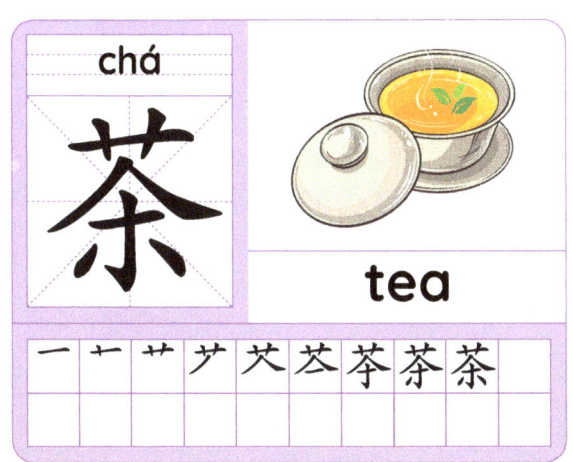

**EXAMPLES**

| 喝茶 | hē chá | to drink tea |
| 倒茶 | dào chá | to pour tea |
| 茶叶 | chá yè | tea leaves |

Radical: 艹　　Strokes: 9

**EXAMPLES**

| 喝酒 | hē jiǔ | to drink wine |
| 倒酒 | dào jiǔ | to pour wine |
| 酒吧 | jiǔ bā | bar |

Radical: 氵　　Strokes: 10

# DRINKS

**EXAMPLES**

| 果汁 | guǒ zhī | juice |
| 多汁 | duō zhī | juicy |
| 橘汁 | jú zhī | orange juice |

Radical: 氵  Strokes: 5

**EXAMPLES**

| 羊奶 | yáng nǎi | goat's milk |
| 奶粉 | nǎi fěn | milk powder |
| 奶奶 | nǎi nai | grandma (paternal) |

Radical: 女  Strokes: 5

# CLOTHES

**EXAMPLES**

| 大衣 | dà yī | coat |
| 上衣 | shàng yī | top (clothes) |
| 衣服 | yī fu | clothes |

Radical: 衣　Strokes: 6

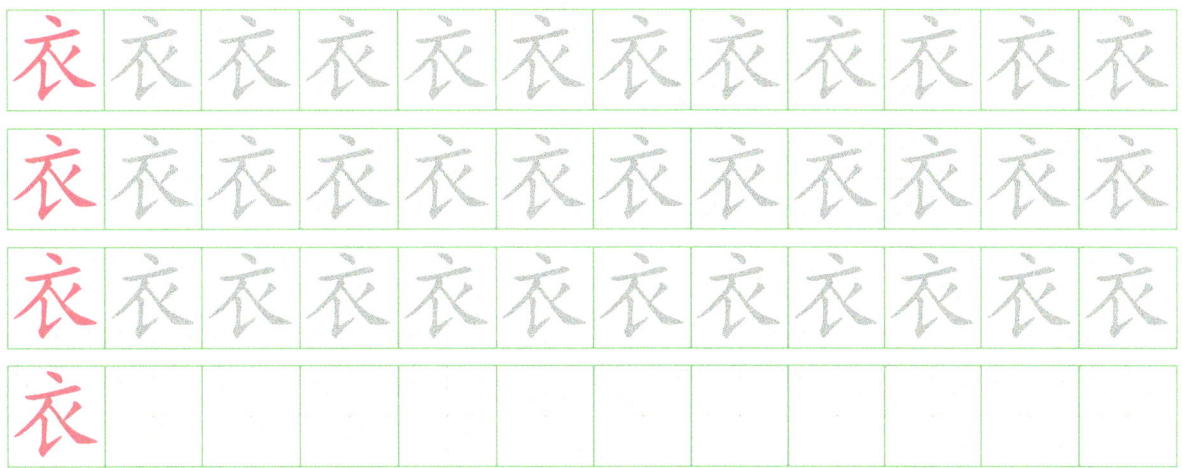

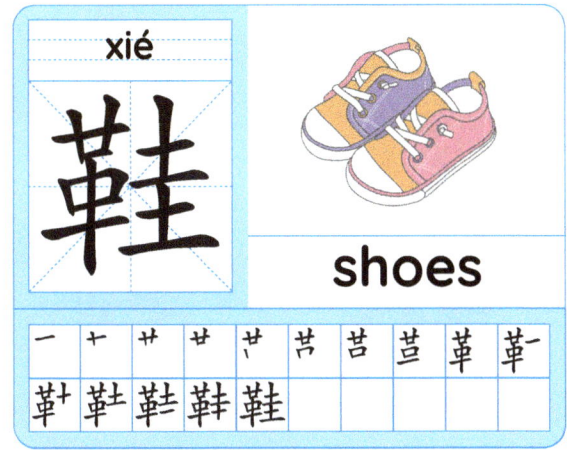

**EXAMPLES**

| 鞋子 | xié zi | shoes |
| 穿鞋 | chuān xié | put on shoes |
| 脱鞋 | tuō xié | take off shoes |

Radical: 革　Strokes: 15

# CLOTHES

**EXAMPLES**

| 裙子 | qún zi | skirt |
| 长裙 | cháng qún | long skirt |
| 短裙 | duǎn qún | short skirt |

Radical: 衤   Strokes: 12

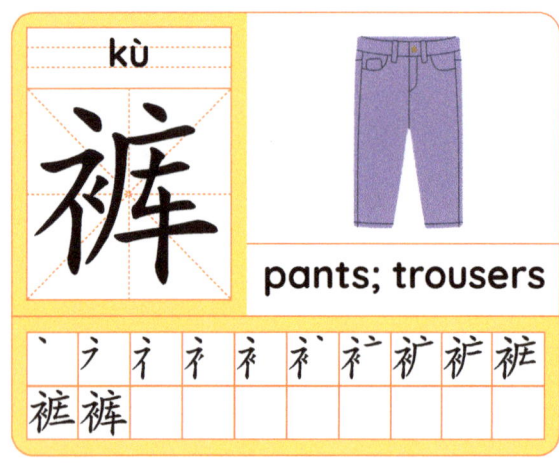

**EXAMPLES**

| 裤子 | kù zi | trousers |
| 裤兜 | kù dōu | pockets (pants) |
| 短裤 | duǎn kù | shorts |

Radical: 衤   Strokes: 12

# CLOTHES

EXAMPLES

| 袜子 | wà zi | socks |
| 腿袜 | tuǐ wà | leg socks |
| 短袜 | duǎn wà | short socks |

Radical: 衤   Strokes: 10

EXAMPLES

| 帽子 | mào zi | hat |
| 草帽 | cǎo mào | straw hat |
| 高帽 | gāo mào | tall hat |

Radical: 巾   Strokes: 12

## SOCIAL RELATIONSHIPS

| | | |
|---|---|---|
| 父亲 | fù qīn | father |
| 父母 | fù mǔ | parents |
| 祖父 | zǔ fù | grandfather |

EXAMPLES

Radical: 父    Strokes: 4

EXAMPLES

| | | |
|---|---|---|
| 母亲 | mǔ qīn | mother |
| 母爱 | mǔ ài | motherly love |
| 祖母 | zǔ mǔ | grandmother |

Radical: 母    Strokes: 5

# SOCIAL RELATIONSHIPS

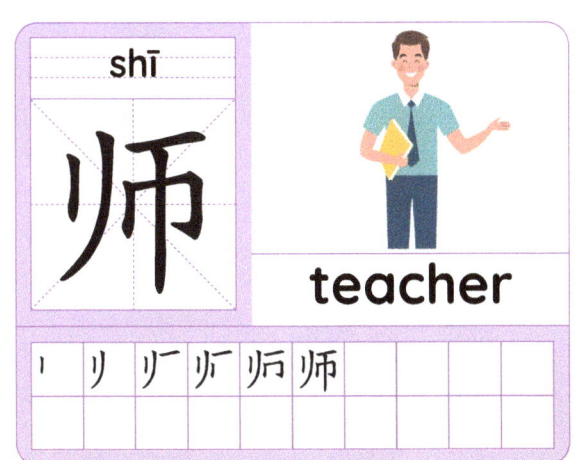

shī

师

teacher

丿 丨 丿 丿 师 师

**EXAMPLES**

| 老师 | lǎo shī | teacher |
| 教师 | jiào shī | school teacher |
| 大师 | dà shī | master |

Radical: 巾　Strokes: 6

shēng

生

student; life

丿 一 ㄙ 生 生

**EXAMPLES**

| 学生 | xué sheng | student |
| 师生 | shī shēng | teachers and students |
| 医生 | yī shēng | doctor |

Radical: 生　Strokes: 5

# SOCIAL RELATIONSHIPS

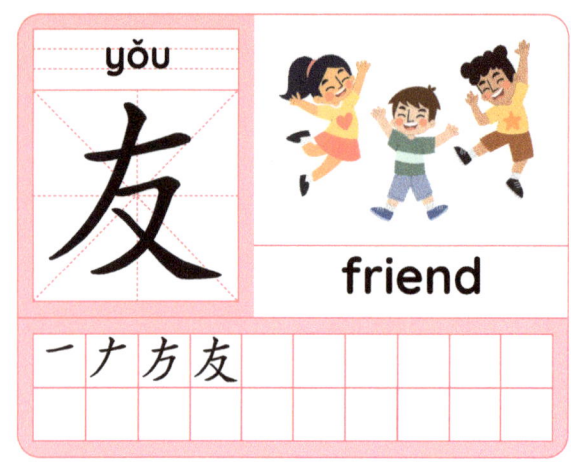

**EXAMPLES**

| 朋友 | péng yǒu | friend |
| 男友 | nán yǒu | boyfriend |
| 女友 | nǚ yǒu | girlfriend |

Radical: 又　Strokes: 4

**EXAMPLES**

| 同学 | tóng xué | classmate |
| 同事 | tóng shì | colleague |
| 同行 | tóng háng | peers |

Radical: 冂　Strokes: 6

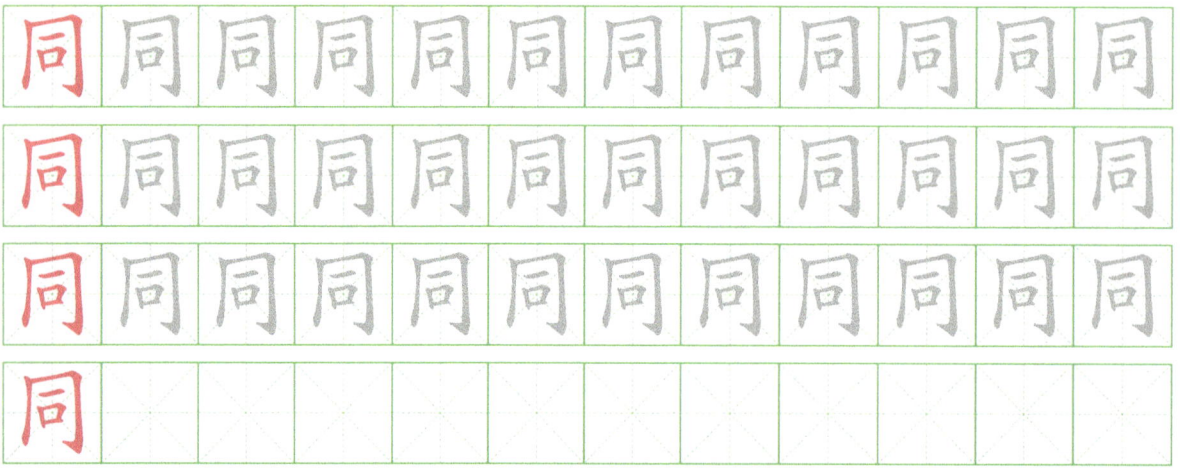

## SOCIAL RELATIONSHIPS

**bàn** — partner

Strokes: ノ 亻 亻 亻 伂 伴 伴

**EXAMPLES**

| 同伴 | tóng bàn | fellow |
| 伙伴 | huǒ bàn | buddy |
| 伴侣 | bàn lǚ | partner (relationship) |

Radical: 亻　Strokes: 7

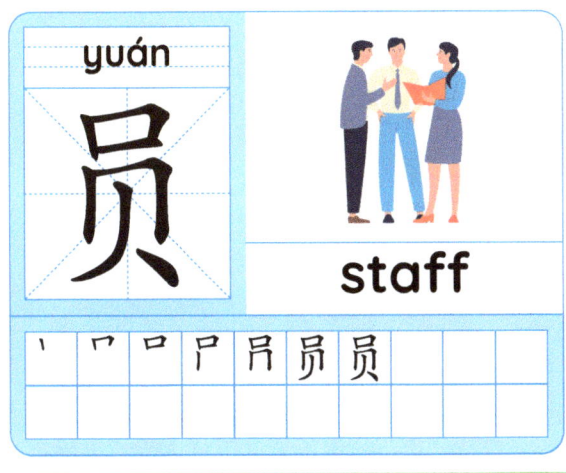

**yuán** — staff

Strokes: ノ 冂 口 尸 吊 员 员

**EXAMPLES**

| 员工 | yuán gōng | employee |
| 会员 | huì yuán | member |
| 职员 | zhí yuán | clerk |

Radical: 口　Strokes: 7

— 73 —

# RESOURCES

## ACCESS AUDIO

1. Scan the QR code
or go to https://linglingmandarin.com/kidswrite3audio

2. Enter the Book Password: **MONKEY88**

## 300 ESSENTIAL CHINESE CHARACTERS WORKBOOK SERIES

Workbook 1
(1 - 100)

Workbook 2
(101 - 200)

Workbook 3
(201 - 300)

# WRITING PRACTICE BOOKS

# BEGINNER BOOKS

LEARN CHINESE VOCABULARY FOR BEGINNERS: NEW HSK 1

CHINESE STORIES FOR LANGUAGE LEARNERS: ELEMENTARY

CHINESE CONVERSATIONS FOR BEGINNERS

LingLing is a native Chinese Mandarin educator with an MA in Communication and Language. Originally from China, now living in the UK, she is the founder of the learning brand LingLing Mandarin, which aims to create the best resources for learners to master the Chinese language and achieve deep insight into Chinese culture in a fun and illuminating way. For more about LingLing and her books, go to www.linglingmandarin.com

www.ingramcontent.com/pod-product-compliance
Lightning Source LLC
Chambersburg PA
CBHW051318110526
44590CB00031B/4393